Rhyme and Analogy

TEACHER'S GUIDE

Oxford

Usha Goswami

with material by Clare Kirtley

Oxford University Press

Oxford University Press, Great Clarendon Street, Oxford OX2 6DP

Oxford   New York
Athens   Auckland Bangkok Bogota Bombay
Buenos Aires   Calcutta   Cape Town   Dar es Salaam   Delhi
Florence   Hong Kong   Istanbul   Karachi
Kuala Lumpur   Madras   Madrid   Melbourne
Mexico City   Nairobi   Paris   Singapore
Taipei   Tokyo   Toronto   Warsaw

and associated companies in
Berlin   Ibadan

Oxford is a trade mark of Oxford University Press

First published 1996
Reprinted 1996, 1997, 1998

ISBN 0 19 916833 4

Typeset and designed by Hardlines, Charlbury, Oxford
Printed in Great Britain

Acknowledgements

Ideas for links with other curriculum areas, activities and games,
and photocopiable resources provided by Clare Kirtley

Illustrations by Jane Bottomley, Alex Brychta (cover), Jan Lewis
Photos by Martin Sookias

Although too numerous to mention individually, the author
would like to thank all the children and teachers in schools in
and around Oxford and Cambridge and elsewhere who so
generously gave their time and enthusiasm to the research on
which the Rhyme and Analogy programme is based.

The author and publisher would also like to thank those
schools around the country who have assisted in trialling the
Rhyme and Analogy materials.

Contents

Contents

Using this Teacher's Guide

This guide is divided into a number of sections. These give:

■ An outline of the research background to the programme and the key teaching aims.

■ An explanation of the programme's components and how they fit together.

■ An explanation of how to play the 'Clue Game'.

■ Detailed sets of notes on how to use each of the individual Story Rhymes.

■ Notes on how to assess learning and progression through the programme.

■ Ideas for activities and games that can be used with every Story Rhyme.

■ A more detailed discussion of the research background to the programme, with suggestions for further reading.

■ A Glossary of terms used in this guide.

■ Clue Card outlines and other photocopiable resources.

Some conventions have been adopted throughout this guide. These are:

■ the use of capital letters (B) to refer to letter *names*

■ the use of lower-case letters in quotation marks ('b') to refer to letter *sounds*

■ the use of italics for emphasis and of inverted commas for clue words noted in the text

■ the use of a listening symbol ⌒ to refer to oral activities

■ the use of a writing symbol ✏ for linking sound to print

■ boxes to show a *summary* of information in the text

■ boxes to show *additional* information

Research background

The Oxford Reading Tree Rhyme and Analogy programme has been designed to help teachers to build on recent research findings about the role of rhyming and analogies in learning to read and to spell. An introduction to the research is given here, with a fuller survey on pp.124 – 7.

Phonological awareness

Recent research has shown that a child's awareness of the sounds in spoken words – *phonological awareness* – is a crucial foundational skill for learning to read. In particular, an awareness of *rhyming* and *alliteration* is important for a child to become a good reader. Rhyming is important for reading because learning to recognise rhyme helps children to understand that any spoken word can be broken down into smaller units of sound. The *smallest* units of sound in words are usually represented by individual alphabetic letters (e.g. the word 'zip' has three constituent sounds, corresponding to the alphabetic letters Z, I, and P). However, the most *psychologically accessible* units of sound in words for the beginning reader are those that make one word rhyme with another.

Linguists call these units *rimes*. The rime of a word like 'zip' is 'ip', and the rime of 'light' is 'ight'. An early focus on rhyme can help children to develop a strong awareness of rime units in spoken words, and this rime awareness necessarily involves the segmentation of initial sounds, too. The beginning sounds in words – those that reflect alliteration – are also very accessible to beginning readers. The linguistic term for these initial units is *onsets*. 'Cat', 'scat', and 'splat' have the onsets 'c', 'sc', and 'spl', respectively.

So words that rhyme sound the same at the end, because they share a rime. They sound different at the beginning, because they have different onsets. The linguistic term 'rime' is used here as a short-hand way of referring to the spelling pattern that reflects the rhyme. The term 'rhyme' is used to mean oral rhymes, which can have different rime spelling patterns, as in 'head' and 'said'. Phonological judgements about whether words begin with the same sound or share rhymes are fairly easy for children, even before they begin school. Judgements that involve smaller units of sound – phonemes – are more difficult. A *phoneme* is the smallest unit of sound that changes the meaning of a word. 'Hot' and 'hat' differ by a single phoneme, the middle phoneme, 'hot' and 'hop' differ by the final phoneme, and 'cat' and 'hat' differ by the initial phoneme.

However, whereas initial phonemes are easy for most children to hear, middle and final phonemes are not. Even six- and seven-year-olds will have difficulty in telling you whether 'hot' and 'hop' share a middle sound, or whether 'tap' and 'hop' end with the same sound. These *phonemic* judgements are very difficult for children until they have attained a certain level of reading, so it is important to begin teaching a child to read at the appropriate developmental level – the level of rhyme and alliteration. Teachers who are particularly interested in the research background will find fuller notes and suggested extension reading at the end of this guide, p. 124.

Onsets and rimes

To segment any syllable into onset and rime, divide at the vowel.

Onset = the sound corresponding to any initial consonants in the syllable.

zip	'z'
drip	'dr'
strip	'str'
parsnip	'p' and 'sn'

Rime = the sound corresponding to the remaining letters of the syllable.

zip, drip, strip	'ip'
parsnip	'ar' and 'ip'
lunchbox	'unch' and 'ox'
at	'at'
end	'end'

Research into the classroom

The early-developing awareness of onsets and rimes provides teachers with a useful starting point for teaching children that we use the alphabet to represent the sounds in words. Onsets are successfully taught by many teachers and alphabet

friezes appear in many classrooms. It can also be straightforward to teach children about rimes, by using *analogies*, as words that share rhyming sounds are often spelled in a similar way (e.g. 'zip', 'nip', 'chip').

These spelling similarities can be used to make *analogies* in reading. If you know one word in a rhyming group (such as 'zip'), then you can make analogies to new words with the same rime, like 'lip', 'nip', and 'chip', and work out that these words will be pronounced to rhyme with 'zip'. You can also use your knowledge of how to write 'zip' to make spelling analogies. If you change the onset of 'zip', you can write rhyming words like 'tip', 'lip', and 'rip'. Rime analogies enable children to begin linking sound to spelling at the most accessible developmental level. However, the first step in teaching analogy skills is to provide a good grounding in the *oral* recognition of onset and rhyme. Good *phonological awareness* is a necessary and important foundation for the development of analogy.

Analogy

To read a word that we don't know

We think of a word that we *do* know.

Analogy = using shared spellings to predict shared sounds (and using shared sounds to predict shared spelling patterns).

zip	→	lip
light	→	fight
sing	→	wing

It is important to note that teaching children correspondences between onsets, rhymes, and spelling patterns is *not* quite the same thing as traditional phonics. More traditional phonic reading schemes are based on the *phoneme*. Their aim is to teach children all the letter–sound correspondences in written English as phonic 'rules'. Children can then blend together the letter–sound correspondences in unknown words, and derive a pronunciation for them. For example, the pronunciation of 'cat' can be derived by blending together the sounds of the letters C, A, and T. The pronunciation of 'strict' can be derived in the same way, from the sounds of the letters S, T, R, I, C, T.

This phonemic approach seems quite natural to an adult who can already read. However, it is not such a good method for *beginning* readers. There are a number of reasons for this:

- Younger children can have great difficulty in hearing the constituent phonemes in spoken words. Phonemes are not readily accessible units of sound to young children, unless they are in the initial position in the word (onset).

- The correspondence between phonemes and alphabetic letters is not straightforward. In some words, such as 'cat' and 'strict', there is a single alphabetic letter for each sound (phoneme). However, in other words, like 'chat', 'cheap', and 'bought', there is not. All of these words are made up of three phonemes.

- Young children have fairly limited acoustic memories. A phonemic approach to reading requires the child to generate each letter–sound correspondence during decoding, and then to retain these sounds in the correct *order* prior to blending. This sequence of requirements can be too much to remember for many children.

This is not to say that all young children will have problems with a phonemic approach. Children who begin school with very well-developed phonological skills can cope with traditional phonics. Most children, however, will not enter school with such skills.

Levels of phonological development

1. syllables
2. onsets and rimes
3. phonemes

Phonological difficulties as an early warning sign

Some children may have severe difficulties in the oral recognition of onsets and rhymes. If you notice a child who is having persistent difficulty in recognising rhyme orally, or who is unable to generate new rhyming words, then this child may be at risk of reading difficulties. Unusual and *persistent* difficulties with the oral tasks are a warning of possible reading problems later on, and if they continue, should be followed up with an expert assessment.

Classroom practice

The main Oxford Reading Tree scheme is based on a 'story experience' or 'whole language' approach to reading. The reason for this is to provide a natural link between children's enjoyment of stories and the printed word. The Rhyme and Analogy programme preserves the story experience approach with the Story Rhymes.

The Story Rhymes are the centrepiece of the Rhyme and Analogy Programme. They provide the focus for developing children's phonological awareness of the sounds of spoken language and for teaching children how these sounds are coded by the alphabet. This helps to develop the use of reading and spelling analogies. The programme thus extends the 'whole language' approach to reading by providing opportunities for the explicit teaching of the links between spelling and sound.

This explicit instruction is necessary in order to help most children become fluent readers (see the National Curriculum). The Story Rhymes are provided in 'Big Book' form and as smaller books for individual reading. The Big Books enable you to 'share' your reading with the class, developing important emergent literacy skills in the children. These skills include understanding the convention that we read from left to right and from top to bottom. Seeing the print also helps the development of informal knowledge about spelling patterns. Although some children learn these pre-reading skills at home by reading with their parents, others do not.

The scheme progresses in twelve Story Rhymes through a carefully-structured set of rhyming word 'families'. The early Story Rhymes focus on simple consonant-vowel-consonant (CVC) rhyme families, like the 'zip' family, the 'pin' family, and the 'hen' family. Later books are based on rhyme families with increasingly difficult letter–sound correspondences, chosen to exemplify so-called 'phonic rules'. These rules include the pronunciation of particular consonant blends and consonant digraphs.

The Story Rhymes also work at multiple levels for children of differing abilities. While the whole class can enjoy listening to a particular Story Rhyme, some groups can then focus on oral activities, while others can work on reading or spelling by analogy. Extension activities are also provided in each Story Rhyme to extend the learning of more able children.

Although best complemented by the popular Oxford Reading Tree stories, the Rhyme and Analogy programme is a complete and independent package for teaching phonological awareness and reading and spelling by analogy. The twelve Story Rhymes and their associated features stand alone to provide the teacher with an integrated and structured package to teach phonological skills and reading by analogy.

Teaching aims of the programme
- To foster children's crucial *phonological awareness*, by focusing their attention on the *sounds* in spoken words, particularly onsets and rhymes.
- To promote an understanding of the *alphabet*, and how it works, first in the context of onsets and rimes, and then by segmenting onsets and rimes into phonemes.
- To develop both *reading* and *spelling* skills, by demonstrating how similarities and differences in sound are linked to similarities and differences in spelling.
- To develop independent learning, by fostering the use of a strategy – *analogy* – that can be extended to many other words that may be encountered during independent reading.

The three key areas are onset, rhyme, rime analogy.

Nursery rhymes

A collection of nursery rhymes is not a formal component of this programme. However, nursery rhymes provide one of the easiest and most enjoyable ways of encouraging children to think about rhyme. Singing and learning nursery rhymes will help your class to consolidate what they learn about rhyme.

Not all nursery rhymes are equal, however: some rhyme, and others do not! You will need to look carefully at the words used in each rhyme. For example, nursery rhymes like *Jack and Jill*, *Humpty Dumpty*, and *Ding dong bell* are largely based on words that do actually rhyme. Nursery rhymes like *Baa baa black sheep*, which rhymes 'dame' with 'lane', *This old man*, which rhymes 'one' with 'thumb', and *Ride a cock horse*, which rhymes 'horse' with 'cross', are not.

The 'non-rhyming' nursery rhymes are important for teaching, as they are a useful source of words that sound as though they might rhyme, but which, when you listen very carefully, do not. This is an important teaching point. You can use these 'non-rhyming' nursery rhymes as a contrast to the 'rhyming' ones. This will help your children to become good judges of rhyme.

A number of suggestions for using nursery rhymes in your classroom are included in the Activities section of this guide (see p. 94). As well as simply reading and singing these rhymes, these include:
- Stopping before the rhyming words and encouraging the children to provide them.
- Changing some of the rhyming words and getting the children to correct you.
- Asking the children to wave every time they hear a word that rhymes with a given word.
- Helping the children to record some of their favourite nursery rhymes on to cassette.
- Getting the children to act out the nursery rhymes with puppets.
- Clapping the rhythm of a rhyme and asking the children to guess which one it is.
- Helping the children to make a book containing their favourite nursery rhymes.
- Introducing the children to number rhymes, and using them to make a number frieze or counting book.

Rhyme anthologies published by Oxford University Press include *Oranges and lemons*, *Ride a cock horse*, *Round and round the garden* (which has a number of counting rhymes), and *Pudding and pie*.

The components of the Rhyme and Analogy programme

Story Rhyme materials

Story Rhymes

There are twelve Story Rhymes, in two packs of six, A and B. Each Story Rhyme focuses on four rhyme families. The Story Rhymes should be read to a whole class or group of children, with a lively rhythm and stress on the rhyming words. See page 95 for a list of the Story Rhymes in order.

Story Rhymes Big Books

The Big Books mean that you can point out key words and spelling patterns to the children, and explicitly model reading by analogy. Detailed instructions on how to do this are given in the sections on each Story Rhyme. The Big Books are identical to the children's Story Rhymes, just enlarged.

Story Rhyme Tapes

The Story Rhyme Tapes are for individual or small-group work, and may also be taken home. There is one tape for each Story Rhyme. The tapes contain the text of each story set to music and some phonological activities involving guessing missing rhymes. Repetition of the stories on the tapes will help to develop acoustic memory as well as phonological awareness and the music emphasizes rhythm, mood and key rhymes. The children can also listen to the tapes and follow the print in the small books at the same time. This helps them to remember the stories, and reinforces spelling knowledge.

Alphabet materials

Alphabet Frieze

The Alphabet Frieze supports onset work. It includes all 26 letters of the alphabet, colour coded by vowel or consonant. The illustrations are carefully picked to be phonologically unambiguous. The digraphs CH, TH, WH, and SH are also featured, and the onsets for the popular ORT characters.

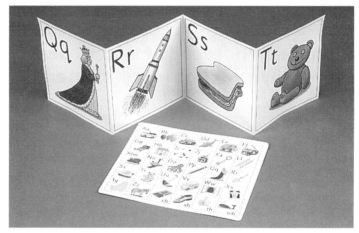

Alphabet Mats

The frieze is also condensed onto tabletop mats for the children to use for personal reference. The mats include the 26 letters and four digraphs.

Activity materials

Card Games

The Card Games support the oral and spelling work that develops from both Alphabet work and the Story Rhymes, and support both onset and rhyme work. They are based on categorising sounds. One set of games (Set 1) develops oral awareness of onsets, and another (Set 3) develops oral awareness of rhymes. The games in Sets 1 and 3 can be played at the same stage of development, as is made clear in the instruction leaflet.

The games in Sets 2 and 4 support the analogy work by linking sound categorisation to categorisation by spelling pattern. Set 2 helps children to link initial sounds to individual letters, and Set 4 helps them to link rhyming sounds to spelling patterns. The games in Sets 2 and 4 can be introduced either when the children learn the Clue Game or as a precursor to the Clue Game (see below).

Alphabet Photocopy Masters and Story Rhyme Photocopy Masters

These are photocopiable activity sheets that have been designed to support the oral and analogy work. The Alphabet Photocopy Masters provide practice in matching letters and sounds, and in tracing and writing letters. The Story Rhyme Photocopy Masters provide practice in categorising rhyming sounds, and in matching rhymes and spelling patterns for

rimes. They include 'listening' activities, coded 'L'; recognising and reading, coded 'RR'; and reading and writing, coded 'RW'. Both include photocopiable sheets that can be used for assessment.

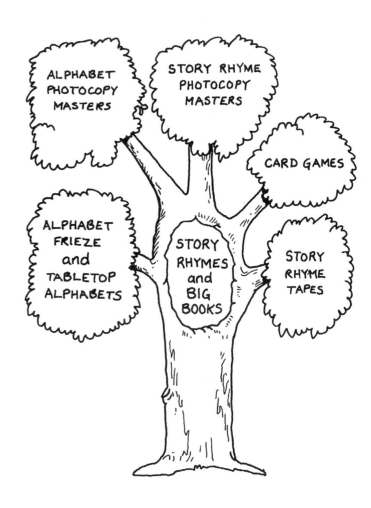

How the different components interlink ▲

The research rationale for this approach is given at the end of this guide (p. 124). Although it is not actually necessary to read the research section in order to use the Rhyme and Analogy programme, it is worth becoming familiar with the background to the programme. An understanding of why the scheme has been designed around rhyme and analogy will not only give you a better insight into how to use it, but will also help you to extend it in ways that may complement the teaching methods that you are already using.

The Clue Game

To read a word that we don't know,
We think of a clue that we *do* know.

The Clue Game teaches children to read and to spell by analogy the words from the different Story Rhymes. It depends on key or 'clue' words from each story, which are provided as Clue Cards (see photocopiable resources, p. 108). The Clue Card words should be cut out, coloured in and mounted on card as each set is learned by reading the relevant Story Rhyme.

These Clue Card words are segmented into onsets and rimes during the Clue Game. New onsets are blended onto shared rimes, using plastic letters (not supplied). This enables explicit modelling of the analogy strategy. After they have been learned, the Clue Cards should be displayed on a wall of the classroom, categorised by *vowel sound*. This is described more fully below. Copies of the Clue Cards can also be made as desk references, and can be used in the games and activities suggested in the section beginning on p. 94.

The Clue Game is a way of modelling the analogy process explicitly. By copying you, the children can learn how to use analogies in their own independent reading and writing. Short and frequent Clue Game sessions are envisaged – perhaps one ten-minute session a day, or one five-minute session in the morning and one after lunch.

The game begins with reading analogies, and progresses to spelling analogies. However, some teachers prefer to begin with spelling analogies, and then to model reading analogies. As the children nominate the words to be spelled, the latter sequence enables a more child-led approach. See what works best for you, as both teaching sequences are equally beneficial.

> You will need some means of displaying spelling patterns, ideally:
>
> an easel, a large magnetic board, and plastic magnetic letters
>
> *or* a 'fuzzy felt' board with 'fuzzy felt' letters
>
> *or* letters made out of strong card, with Blu-tack or Velcro on the back to attach them to a white-board or a cloth board
>
> *or* large flip-sheets, on which you can write the onsets and rimes in coloured pens

The children will need access to the letters, and plastic letters are best as they can be *physically manipulated*. This is especially important for slower learners. If the children are allowed to handle the letters themselves, it can make a real difference to reading progress by introducing a multi-sensory approach. The children will need quite a lot of letters as they get good at the game.

How to play the game

A good way to begin the Clue Game is to cut out and colour the relevant Clue Cards as a class activity. You will need a 'master' copy of each clue word, coloured and mounted on card, and covered with sticky-back plastic.

Begin the game by showing the children the Clue Card for the rhyme family that you are going to teach (e.g. 'net'). Ask them to read it for you. They should always be able to read the Clue Cards because of the picture prompts. Then attach the Clue Card to the top of the magnetic board. Talk the children through what you are doing, asking them to tell you which letters you will need to make up the clue word. You could say:

> We can use the clue card to tell us which letters we need to write 'net'. Which ones are they? That's right, we need N, E and T. I'm going to spell 'net' for you here in plastic letters.
>
> Look, I'm leaving a gap in my spelling. Why am I doing that? Yes, because there are two parts to 'net' the 'n' sound, which is spelled with . . . ? (children = N), and the 'et' sound which is spelled with . . . ? (children = E, T).

The gap separates the onset and the rime. The segmented rime can then be used as a basis for analogies. Lists of rhyme family words are provided at the end of each Story Rhyme section.

Reading analogies

A reading analogy involves reading new words by using the rime from the clue word. For example, the children can use 'net' as a basis for reading 'jet'. Always line up the onsets and the rimes of new words to be read, leaving a gap between onset and rime.

For example, you could add new words for the

children to read one by one, so that you build up a list of analogous spellings (all with aligned rimes). You might begin by adding the word 'jet', leaving a gap so that you write it? J – ET. You could say something like:

> Now I want you to use your clue word to try and read this new word for me. What letters am I using? That's right, J, E, T. What word do you think that J,E,T might spell?

> Good work! Yes, this new word is 'jet'! Do you know how we tell? We check with our clue. What does this bit of the word say? (*pointing to the rime*). It's the same in both words. That's right, the letters E,T make the sound 'et'. They make the 'et' sound in 'jet' and the 'et' sound in 'net'.

> So to figure out 'jet', how can we use 'net' as a clue? That's right, we can match their rimes. Look, 'n-et', 'j-et'.

It is always useful to go through the analogy process for the children, even if they have got the new word right. This is good reinforcement.

You can also model using the Alphabet Frieze to work out onsets.

> If we don't know the sound for J, what can we do? That's right, we can use the alphabet frieze to help us. The picture that goes with J is the picture of some . . . ? (jam). What is the first sound in 'jam'? Yes, 'j'.

> So we know the sound for J, which is? Yes, 'j', and we know the sound for the pattern E,T from the clue word, which is?

> Yes, 'et'. So the new word is? Yes, it's 'j-et' (*demonstrating how to blend the onset to the rime*). So if we know 'net', we can work out how to read 'jet', because they rhyme – 'n-et', 'j-et'. Remember:

> > To read a word that we don't know,
> > We think of a clue that we *do* know.

Now ask the children to think up some rhyming words for you to make. Then ask them to work out

which ones you are making, by using analogies. Alternatively, you can add more words to the board for the children to read yourself ('wet', 'yet', 'set', etc.). Always model the Clue Game procedure after each analogy is made. The more repetition, the better!

Extension work

Once you have modelled the analogy strategy a number of times for the children, let them take it in turns to adopt the role of the teacher. Now they have to explain to the other children how to make an analogy. To begin with, it is probably wise for you to choose the analogy words for the 'teacher' to use. However, once the children are familiar with the Clue Game, they can do this themselves. Make sure that the 'teacher' teaches the others how they should be using the clue. Having to explain something to someone else is one of the best ways of consolidating learning.

Another extension activity is to use words of more than one syllable that share the taught rime (e.g. carp*et*, l*et*ter). This extension activity can be introduced once the children are thoroughly familiar with the Clue Game. Instructions on how to play the Clue Game with longer words are given at the end of some of the Story Rhyme sections, beginning with Story Rhyme 5 (see p. 45).

Spelling analogies

> To spell a word that we don't know,
> We think of a clue that we *do* know.

In spelling analogies, we use the clue word to choose the correct letters to *spell* new words. The clue word tells the child about rhyming spellings. Thus, for analogies in spelling the teacher simply reverses the procedure for analogies in reading.

A good way to begin the Clue Game for spelling is to place the Clue Card at the top of the board, as before, and ask the children which letters you will need to spell it. Then ask them how you would *write* a new word that rhymes with the clue. You could follow the pattern described for reading analogies and then say:

> Now, I'm thinking of a word that rhymes with 'net'. My word is 'wet'. Can you use the clue word to work out how to write 'wet' for me?

As usual, model the analogy process explicitly for the children, using open-ended questions, even if they get the new spellings right. This is good reinforcement. You could say something like:

Good work! Yes, we spell 'wet' W, E, T, and how do we know?

Which sound is the same in both words? Yes, 'et', which is the rhyming sound. You can hear it – 'n-et', 'w-et'.

So if the words *sound* the same, what do we know about their spellings? Yes, they should have the *same* letters. So we can tell how to write the 'et' sound from our clue. Which letters will we need? Yes, that's right – E, T.

So it is easy to work out how to spell 'wet', because we can use 'net' as a clue. We already know how to write the 'et' part of 'wet' (*pointing to the shared rime, and comparing the two 'ET's*). We just need the letter for the 'w' sound, which is . . . ? Yes, W.

You can use a discussion about onset spellings to practise phonological awareness of onsets:

If we don't know the letter for the 'w' sound, what can we do? That's right, we can think of other words with the 'w' sound at the beginning, that we can already write. Can you think of any? (*Providing an opportunity to think about alliteration*).

Alternatively, you can model the use of the Alphabet Frieze to work out onsets.

What else can we do to find the letter for the 'w' sound? Yes, we can find out how to write the sound from the Alphabet Frieze. Can you see another word on the frieze that begins with the same sound as 'wet'? Yes, its 'window'.

So we know the letter to write the first sound 'w' in 'wet', don't we? What is it? Yes, its W, and we know the letters for the rhyming sound 'et' already, don't we? What are they? Yes, they are E, T. It's just like the pattern in our clue.

So if we know 'net', we can work out how to spell 'wet'. 'Net' is . . . ? Yes, N-E-T and 'wet' is . . . ? Yes, W-E-T. Remember,

To spell a word that we don't know,
We think of a clue that we *do* know.

Now you can ask the children to think up other rhyming words that they would like to spell. Don't worry if they come up with longer words, such as 'carpet'. Use the clue to spell the shared rime 'et', and either add the letters for the first syllable without comment, or, if the children are quite familiar with the Clue Game, use analogies. Ask them to think of clues for writing the first rime (e.g. car: bar, star, far). As each analogy is made, always model the Clue Game process. Repetition never hurts!

Extension work

Once you have modelled the analogy strategy a number of times, let the children take it in turns to be the teacher. They can ask the other children to think of words to write, and then they can explain the analogy process to the rest of the group. With spelling analogies, you can even leave the children to spell a whole series of words by analogy on their own – you can check for errors after the group has reached a consensus on each spelling, as the evidence will be displayed on the board.

Multisyllabic words can also be used to extend practice in spelling by analogy – see individual sections at the end of some of the Story Rhymes, beginning with Story Rhyme 5 (p. 45).

The summary checklist for the Clue Game is also provided as a photocopiable sheet – see p. 106.

Finally, the basic Clue Game can be extended to cover any other rhyme families that you may wish to teach, or that the children want to learn. These rhyme families might arise from a particular class project, for example, or from other school activities.

The Clue Game: summary checklist
- Put the Clue Card at the top of the board.
- Make the clue word from plastic letters, separating onset and rime.

Reading
- Add a new rhyming word, separated into onset and rime, lining up the spelling pattern with the clue word.
- Ask the children for the sound of the onset (they can use the Alphabet Frieze).
- Ask the children for the sound of the rime (they can use the clue word).
- Ask them to read the new word for you.
- Ask them how they can check that they are right (they can use analogies).

Spelling
- Ask the children for a new word to spell.
- Ask them how to write its rime (they can use the clue word).
- Ask them how to write the onset (they can use the Alphabet Frieze).
- Ask them how they can check that they are right (they can use analogies).

Displaying the Clue Cards

The Clue Cards from each Story Rhyme need to be displayed on a wall in the classroom. It is important to ensure that their spelling patterns are constantly available to the children, to encourage their use as clues when the children are reading and writing on their own. The children need a permanent reference point that they can use when they come across spelling patterns that they need to match to a clue word.

There are many possibilities for this display, all of which can be made by the children themselves as a class activity. A Word Tree is the suggested method of display, because it extends the tree metaphor underlying Oxford Reading Tree. However, any other display method can also be used, as long as it enables the five vowels to be categorised separately, colour-coded by vowel. The children can also make individual copies of the Clue Cards being used at any given time to use as a desk resource.

How to make a Word Tree

A simple tree can be made out of sugar paper. It can be painted by the children, and should have five branches, one for each vowel. The branches can be colour-coded to the Clue Cards, which should be given differently coloured borders. For example, the Clue Cards for A could have red borders, the Clue Cards for E could have yellow borders, the Clue Cards for I could have blue borders, the Clue Cards for O could have green borders, and the Clue Cards for U could have orange borders. If you match the colour of the tree branches to these colours, then children who remove a Clue Card from the tree will always know which branch it came from.

The vowel-based grouping of the clue words is important for both reading analogies and spelling analogies. When children come across an unfamiliar word in their reading, they can see the vowel/s in the rime, and will thus know immediately which branch of the tree to search for a matching clue word. When the children are trying to write a word, they can go and search for a clue word with the same rime on the basis of its sound.

Although studies of phonological awareness have shown that children have difficulty in distinguishing vowel sounds orally, most of the clue words in the Story Rhymes have fairly distinct vowels. A child looking for the Clue Card 'zip' would probably decide to search the I branch rather than the O or U branches, for example. A child looking for 'fan' would probably

search the A branch or perhaps the A and E branches. The need to search for Clue Cards by vowel will help to develop children's awareness of the vowel sounds. However, the main reason for grouping the Clue Cards by their vowels is to reinforce the onset–rime segmentation strategy necessary for analogies.

Once it has been practised in the Clue Game, each Clue Card should be hung on the correct branch of the tree. The cards must be hung up so that each spelling pattern is clearly visible. As you learn more Story Rhymes, the branches may begin to get a bit full. At this point, the children could begin to create individual Clue Dictionaries to record the spelling patterns of clues that no longer fit onto the Word Tree.

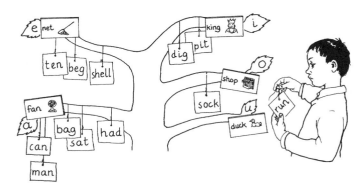

Other display methods

■ The children could make large cut-out shapes of each vowel from sugar paper, and paint them the different vowel colours. The relevant Clue Cards can then be attached (e.g. with Blu-tac) around each vowel.

■ The children could make a wall frieze with five big boxes on it, one for each vowel in the different vowel colours. Each Clue Card can then be attached to the correct box.

■ The children could make a class Clue Dictionary, with five pages of different colours, one for each vowel. This could be hung on the wall, so that all five pages are showing.

■ The children could make individual Clue Dictionaries for themselves. These could have five long pages, one for each vowel. However, it is preferable if these individual dictionaries are *supplementary* to a wall display. The children are more likely to use the clues if their spelling patterns are readily available.

The important constraint for any display method is to *group the clue words by the first vowel in their rimes*. This facilitates easy access to required spellings. The children are being taught to segment any syllable into its constituent onsets and rimes, and so the rime spellings *must* be coded by initial vowel.

The Story Rhymes

The Story Rhymes are the centrepiece of the Rhyme and Analogy programme. They provide a lively context for introducing work on sounds and on spelling. Each Story Rhyme has been written to provide an initial context for work at *either* of these levels with children of different abilities. Some children will continue to need to focus at the oral level with each Story Rhyme, in order to build up good phonological skills. Other children, who may already have good phonological awareness, can use the stories as a basis for reading and spelling by analogy.

The progression in the programme comes from the different rhyme families that form the basis for each Story Rhyme. The activities that develop from each Story Rhyme are the same, but the rhyme patterns on which they are based become more difficult. Early Story Rhymes are written around simple consonant-vowel-consonant (CVC) rhymes like 'net' and 'zip'. These rhyme families provide practice with single-phoneme onsets like 'n' and 'z', and with simple rimes like 'et' and 'ip'. Later Story Rhymes introduce more complex rhyme patterns like 'bell' (CVCC), 'crab' (CCVC), and 'flash' (CCVCC). These rhyme families provide practice with double-consonant onsets like 'cr' and 'fl', and with more complex rimes like 'ell' and 'ash'.

With every Story Rhyme, the key goal for the teacher is to make the children very familiar with the rhyme families in each story. This familiarity begins at the oral level, and covers both onsets and rhymes. Once the children are thoroughly at home with the sounds of the onsets and the rhymes in each story, they learn how shared sounds are reflected in shared spellings (rimes). This is taught through instruction in analogy, using the Clue Game (see p. 11). The Clue Game operates on the following principle:

> To read a word that we don't know,
> We think of a clue that we *do* know.

The principle of *clue words* works for both onsets and rimes. Shared initial sounds predict shared spelling (cap, cot, car; Floppy, flap, fly) in the same way as shared rhyming sounds do (zip, nip, rip). Clue words can also be used to read longer words by thinking of a clue for each syllable. A long word like 'fingertip' doesn't look so difficult when 'fing' is compared to 'king', 'er' to 'her', and 'tip' to 'zip'.

Using the Story Rhymes

With any Story Rhyme, the teaching sequence should always begin by familiarising the children with the story. It is important to make sure that they understand the narrative, and appreciate its rhythmic patterning and its humour.

This is best achieved with the Big Books. These have been designed so that the whole class can see the spelling patterns of the words in the story. The teacher can point to the words and the pictures, and guide work on the narrative and phonological patterns. With repeated readings, she can use the Big Book to cover up key rhyming words for the children to call out, and generally reinforce the rhyme patterns in the story. Specific suggestions for reinforcement are given in the teaching notes to each Story Rhyme

Big Book work can then be used as a context for further work on *sound*. This phonological work begins at the oral level, with work on both onsets and rhymes. Ideas for oral work are illustrated with the listening symbol. Oral work on onsets and rhymes is then linked to spelling, and eventually to analogy using the Clue Game (see p. 11). Ideas for linking oral work to spelling are illustrated with the writing symbol ( ).

To illustrate how to use the Story Rhymes in this way, a very detailed teaching sequence is given for the first Story Rhyme, *Supersonic engine juice*. The same basic principles apply to all of the Story Rhymes, however, and so later stories are covered in less detail. These same principles can also be applied to any other story or poem that you might want to use with your class as a basis for analogies.

A summary checklist of how to use the Story Rhymes is given on the next page and is also provided as a photocopiable resource (see p. 105).

The Story Rhymes: summary checklist

1 Begin with the Big Books

■ Read through the Story Rhyme, emphasising the rhymes. Point to the spelling patterns, and any rhymes in pictures.

■ Go through the story more slowly, verse by verse. Focus on the rhyming words, using guided response questions.

■ Check comprehension of the narrative structure, using guided response questions.

■ Reinforce the phonological patterns in the Story Rhymes, in the sequence onset, rhyme, analogy.

2 Onset work

■ Begin with oral work based on the the Story Rhyme.

■ Extend by linking sounds to letters.

3 Rhyme work

■ Begin with oral work based on the Story Rhyme.

■ Extend by linking sounds to letters.

4 Using analogies

■ Play the Clue Game.

■ Extend by using the word family approach and segmenting longer words into syllables.

5 Link to other curriculum areas

Shared reading at home

Encouraging the children to take the Story Rhymes home to share with their parents or other adult carers has a number of benefits. First of all, there is a simple motivational effect – parental interest has been shown to help a child's reading development even when a child is reading to a parent who does not speak English. Parents who can read the Story Rhymes with their children will be able to help the teacher on a number of other levels, too:

■ By reinforcing the child's understanding of oral rhyme ( ).

■ By reinforcing the child's understanding of how spelling and sound are linked ( ).

■ By reinforcing the child's ability to use analogies ( ).

Three sample letters asking parents to provide reinforcement at these three different levels (, ,)are provided as photocopiable resources (see pp. 102 – 4). However, you could also ask parents to provide general practice in rhyme and alliteration, for example by playing games like 'I Spy' at home.

The Story Rhyme Tapes can also be used at home. Parents can join their children in the rhyme exercises at the end of each Story Tape, which will be very motivating for the children. The repetition of the Story Rhymes with parents, either via print or via the tapes, will help the children to remember the rhyme patterns in the stories.

Finally, classroom assistants can also work with individual children in the different ways suggested above and in the letters to parents.

Supersonic engine juice focuses the children's attention on the **net**, **zip**, **fan**, and **tub** rhyme families.

A list of rhyme family words is given on p. 24.

Introducing the Story Rhyme

Supersonic engine juice is about a show-off who gets his come-uppance. The flashy McGinty has a smart speedboat, and he beats the other boats every time. Little Alex has no smart speedboat, and few resources. By using junk, Alex manages to construct a makeshift boat based on an old washing tub. He builds a home-made motor for it, and uses his extra special petrol. McGinty can hardly hide his triumph as the two begin to race, but Alex's little tub speeds past him and wins the day. McGinty ends up sinking, and has to be rescued by Alex.

Begin by reading *Supersonic engine juice* to the children, preferably from the Big Book. Read it more than once, with lively emphasis on the rhythm and the rhyme. Encourage the children to chant the rhyming refrains with you as the story becomes familiar.

>   McGinty's boat was fast it used to
>   [children join] zip, zip, zip
>   Around the bay McGinty loved to
>   [children join] nip, nip, nip

Use the Big Book to show the children both the pictures and the print. Make sure that you point to the rhyming words as you read them, as this will focus the children's attention on how the rhyming words are spelled.

Then work more slowly through the story, verse by verse. Your goal is to make the children think about the sounds of the words that rhyme. They really need to listen to those words, look at their spelling patterns, and think about why they sound the same. Try to increase the children's listening attention when you say the rhyming words by making them sound exciting, exaggerating your intonation. Try to focus their visual attention on the spelling patterns of the rhymes, by continually pointing them out as you read.

For example, as you read the first verse, you could show them McGinty's boat in the picture, and trace an imaginary and speedy trail as you say 'zip, zip, zip' and 'nip, nip, nip'. You could ask them what else zips and nips along (e.g. people on skis, a motorbike, insects, birds). In the second verse, you could point out the jet. You could ask the children what else needs a jet to make it move (an aeroplane, a hovercraft). Stress the word repeatedly, so that the sound pattern is emphasised (e.g. 'a motorboat *jet*, an aeroplane *jet*, a hovercraft *jet* – they all help us to go jet, jet, jetting along!').

Now focus exclusively on the sounds of the rhyming words. Ask the children guided response questions:
- Which words sound like 'zip'? Can you hear them?
- Which words sound like each other on this page?
- Which words rhyme in this bit of the story?

Go through the story again, asking them to listen out for rhymes for 'zip'. If they miss one, point it out yourself. Ask them 'Can you think of any more words that rhyme with 'zip'? Can you make some up?' Nominate some yourself (see list on p. 24).

If the children make mistakes, use these as a teaching point. For example, if a child thinks that 'jet' rhymes with 'zip', you can say:

> Good try, but 'jet' doesn't really sound like 'zip' if we listen carefully, does it? Listen hard: 'z–ip' 'j–et'. Which sounds can you hear at the end? 'Zip' has an . . . ? Yes, an 'ip' sound at the end. 'Jet' has an . . . ? Yes, an 'et' sound. So 'jet' is in a different rhyme family to 'zip'.

If the children suggest rhyming words of more than one syllable, like 'parsnip', use this as a teaching point, too (see p. 47, SR 5). Tell them about syllables. Say something like:

> That's a great word! 'Parsnip' does sound like 'zip', because it rhymes at the end. There are two bits in 'parsnip', though, aren't there? What are they? That's right, *'par-snip'*. Which bit rhymes with 'zip'? That's right, the 'snip' part rhymes with 'zip'. Well done! Are there any other longer rhymes for 'zip'?

When the children become more skilled at rhyming, you could even ask questions like:

> Can anyone think of any rhymes for the first part of 'par-snip'? What else rhymes with 'par'? Are there some good rhymes for 'par'? (Car, star, etc.)

Repeat these activities for the other rhyme families (net, fan, tub).

Checking narrative comprehension

It's also useful to talk more generally about the story, to check the children's comprehension of the narrative structure. Ask them questions like:

- What did Alex use to make a boat? Do we usually make boats out of old washing tubs? Why not?
- Why did McGinty think that he would beat Alex? Was McGinty nice to Alex? Why not?
- Why did Alex's boat go faster than McGinty's? What was Alex's plan? What was his secret weapon?
- What happened to McGinty's boat? What sounds did it make as it crashed?
- Why did Alex have to tow McGinty back to shore? What do you think McGinty felt like when Alex helped him?

You can reinforce the story and the rhyme families by making links with other areas of the curriculum (see ideas at the end of this section). The Story Rhyme Photocopy Masters include a two-page section of activities that can be used to check comprehension of any of the Story Rhymes.

Links to other ORT stories

If possible, discuss other stories where someone shows off and lives to regret it, where there is a race, or boat trip, or where an ingenious invention is made out of scrap. Some suggestions from ORT are: *Kipper the clown*, *The go-kart*, *Nobody got wet*, *Poor old Mum!* and *The great race*.

Developing phonological awareness

Follow the sequence onset, rhyme, analogy

This initial rhyming work should now be reinforced in a number of ways. The activities to reinforce each Story Rhyme are always given in the order *onset, rhyme, analogy*, because this is the easiest sequence for the children to follow. However, some teachers prefer to follow general teaching sessions on the Story Rhyme with the Rhyme activities rather than with the Onset activities, and to cover onsets after dealing with rhymes. This is a matter of choice. The only fixed position in the teaching sequence is that analogy comes last, because it is difficult to use spelling (rime) analogies if you are unsure about how to write onsets.

Reinforcement activities to develop phonological awareness of the stories can include the following:

- Encourage the children to listen to the Story Rhyme Tapes in a quiet corner of the classroom. They should join in with the activities on the tape, for example by filling in the missing rhyming words in the second reading of the story. They can also take the tapes home.

- Let the children listen to the Story Rhyme Tapes with a copy of the Story Rhyme in front of them. Tell them to try and follow the story on tape in the book, turning the pages at the right time by using the page-turn signal. Even if the children cannot follow the print, the pictures will help them to keep up. As they become more skilled, you can ask them to point to the words with a finger as they listen to the tapes.

- Send the individual books of the Story Rhyme home for parents to read with their children. Sample activities for parents to use to support the Rhyme and Analogy work are given on pp. 102 – 4.

- Cover up every second rhyming word in the verses that use the rhyming family words with Post-it notes. Ask the children to supply the missing words as you read, and then uncover the spelling patterns to show them whether they were right or not. As the children become more familiar with the story, you could cover up every rhyming word.

- Let the children play at 'being the teacher' with the Big Book. The story is so short that most children should be able to remember it after some practice, even if they cannot read the print, and the pictures will help to prompt their memories. Allow the 'teacher' to read the Big Book to the rest of the group, pointing out the rhyming refrains and asking the other children to nominate members of the rhyme families. It doesn't matter if the 'teachers' copy exactly what you do – having to teach someone else is a very valuable way of reinforcing learning. They could even use the Post-it notes by themselves.

Some of these ideas for reinforcement are probably best done in small groups. You can then develop this awareness with work that focuses specifically on onsets, rhymes, and analogies.

Onset work

> It may be less confusing for some children if onsets are considered separately from rhymes.

> Salient onsets in *Supersonic engine juice* are
> **z n j y f w c p sh pl gr dr fl**

The key goal of onset work is to make the children concentrate on the initial sounds in words. Several onsets are stressed by the rhyme patterns in *Supersonic engine juice*. The most salient are shown above, and include the double-consonant onsets 'pl', 'gr', 'dr', and 'fl'. All of these onsets can be used for oral practice in listening to shared initial sounds.

For example, you could take up the Big Book, and tell the children that this time their job is to listen out for the *beginning* sounds in the story. Guide their listening in the following ways:
- Read the first verse. Pause, and ask them what the beginning sound is in 'zip', 'zip', 'zip'.
- Ask them to tell you some other words that begin with the 'z' sound.
- Point out 'zebra' on the Alphabet Frieze.
- Ask them what letter they would need to write the 'z' sound.
- Then ask them what the beginning sound is in 'nip', 'nip', 'nip'.
- Ask them to tell you some other words that begin with the 'n' sound.
- Point out 'nest' on the Alphabet Frieze.

- Ask them what letter they would need to write the 'n' sound.

These activities can be continued for all of the key initial sounds in the story. At this stage, keep the onset work at an *oral* level. You can mention the letter names that spell single sounds from the Alphabet Frieze, namely Z, N, J, Y, F, W, C, P, and SH, but the focus should remain on the sounds themselves. There is no need to work on spelling the blends like 'pl' and 'dr', as these will be covered in later Story Rhymes. Of course, as 'fl' and 'gr' are on the Alphabet Frieze (*Floppy* and *Gran*), you can also ask the children which letters you would need to write these onsets.

Reinforcing the onset work

This oral work can then be supplemented in a number of ways, using the Alphabet Frieze, the Tabletop Alphabets, the Alphabet Photocopy Masters, and the Card Games. Some suggestions for reinforcement are given below. The suggestions do not cover all of the onsets in the Story Rhyme, but can easily be extended to do so if you wish. There is no need to practise every onset before going on to the next Story Rhyme, however, as many will occur again.

Any of the other ideas in the Onset section (p. 94) can also be adapted to the particular onsets used in *Supersonic engine juice*. Similarly, any of the Card Games in Set 1 can be played, choosing games at an appropriate developmental level.
- The children can come up with a series of adjectives beginning with 'w', that can all describe Wilma (wonderful Wilma, wet Wilma, warm Wilma). Alternatively, the children can think of a series of things that happen to Wilma: Wilma is walking; Wilma is wishing; Wilma is wondering, etc.
- The children can make a display of objects beginning with the letter F, finding things in the classroom and bringing in items from home. They could use a fork, a felt-tip pen, a number five, a toy fish, a film, etc.
- The children can make a frieze for the letter J that is related to food. They could draw pictures of jelly, jam, juice, etc.
- The children can play an 'add a word' game. Gran went on holiday and she took – *g*rey socks, *g*reen shoes, a *g*reat big towel, a *g*rotty bag, etc.

Extension work

Extend the oral work to letters:

Make Z the letter of the week. The children can make the letter out of wool, string, clay, plasticine, they can write it in paint or felt-tip pen, they can trace it in sand. They can make models of zebras, or paint pictures of zoos.

The children can paint pictures of Wilma's activities (e.g. Wilma is walking, wet Wilma). They can write or trace the appropriate sentences onto the pictures, using big and colourful Ws for the onsets. They can add the Letter Card for F to the display of objects. They can paint a big J onto the food frieze.

The children can find the Sound Picture Cards for F, W, and J. The children can make a large cut-out of a fire-engine, a window, and a jam jar from sugar paper, and write the letters F, W, and J onto the correct pictures. Then they can put the Sound Picture Cards onto the right picture by matching their beginning sound.

Introduce the children to a handpuppet called Nadim, who has a large N pinned to his clothing. Give them the Sound Picture Cards for N along with a selection of three or four others. Ask them to find the pictures that Nadim likes because they begin with the same sound and letter as his name.

The children can make a class book for the letter P. Pencil begins with P. Paint begins with P. Pocket begins with P . . .

Obviously, these activities can be extended to any of the other onsets in *Supersonic engine juice*. You can also ask the children to play some of the Card Games in Set 3, or use some of the activities at the end of the Onset section that involve letters. You can get them to trace the letters on the relevant Alphabet Photocopy Masters, and give them the associated activities for further consolidation and assessment.

Rhyme work

> It may be less confusing for some children if rhymes are considered separately from onsets. The key goal of rhyme work is to make the children focus on rhyming sounds, particularly the rhyme families in the Story Rhyme.

As the initial readings of *Supersonic engine juice* from the Big Book have already focused the children's attention on rhyme, you can now extend this work in a more formal way. Read the story once again with the children, emphasising the rhyming patterns by using the devices of intonation and stress etc. as mentioned previously. Ask them if they can remember the rhymes that they thought of for each clue word (zip, net, fan, tub).

Reinforcing the rhyme work

Now supplement this informal work with other rhyming activities. There are many ideas in the Rhyme section (p. 97) which can be adapted to the rhymes in *Supersonic engine juice*, and any of the Card Games in Set 2 can be played, choosing games at an appropriate developmental level. The rhyme activities in the Story Rhyme Photocopy Masters can also be used; many are based on aural recognition of rhyme (coded 'L').

Play a guided version of rhyming 'I Spy' with your class, in which the teacher uses different rhymes to cue objects in the classroom. 'I'm thinking of something that rhymes with 'hair' (chair). I'm thinking of something that rhymes with 'cable' (table). I'm thinking of something that rhymes with 'talk' (chalk).'

Put some objects into a 'feely bag'. The children take it in turns to withdraw an object, and to suggest something that rhymes with it. Useful objects for the bag include a ball, a spoon, a mug, a hat, a net, a lid, a nut, a pen, etc.

The children can make a rhyming list of activities. 'I was feeling hot so I bought a 'fan'. I went to the seaside and got a 'tan'. I went to the shops and saw a 'man'.'

Put a Rhyme Picture Card from the 'zip' family by the door of the classroom or homebay (zip, lip, chip, ship). The children have to say a word that rhymes with the picture before they go through.

Use the Rhyme Picture Cards from the 'fan' and 'zip' families. The children make big pictures of a 'ship' and a 'man' out of sugar paper. Spread the cards face-up on the table, and ask the children to sort the cards onto the pictures that rhyme.

Extension work

Extend the oral work to rime spellings:

Give the children the Clue Card for 'zip'. Put the Rhyme Picture Cards and the Rhyme Word Cards for 'zip' on the table. The children have to match the Picture Cards to the correct Word Cards. Repeat the activity for 'fan'.

The children can paint pictures of the different rhyming activities that they thought of in the oral work ('I went to the seaside and got a 'tan''). They can write the corresponding sentence onto each picture. Let them use red pen for the rhyme family words, so that the rhyming spelling patterns stand out in the picture display.

Each child can pick an object from the 'feely bag'. They can draw a picture of their object, write its name, and draw a picture of something that rhymes with it.

The children can draw pictures of the rhymes that came up in rhyming 'I Spy'. They can attach the pictures to the rhyming objects (e.g. they can attach the picture of 'hair' to a chair, 'cable' to a table, and so on). Then they can make labels for the objects and the rhyming pictures.

There are a number of other activities at the end of the Rhyme section which involve spelling patterns, and these can also be used for extension work. The Story Rhyme Photocopy Masters also have a couple of activities that involve rime spellings. You can also let the children play some of the Card Games in Set 4.

Using analogies

> To read a word that we don't know,
> We think of a clue that we *do* know.

Analogy simply means teaching children to use the shared spelling patterns in rhyming words in a strategic way to read and to spell new words. The best way to teach analogy is via the Clue Game (see p. 11). The Clue Game focuses on rime analogies. There is no special game for onset analogies, because children will learn about most onsets as they learn to read and to spell different rimes. However, you can use the Clue Game for double-consonant onsets, like 'fl' and 'gr'. Guidelines for adapting the Clue Game to these onsets are provided in Story Rhyme 3 (p. 31).

> The Clue Game should always be played on separate days for different rhyme families.

The Clue Game is always played on separate days for different rhyme families, to avoid confusion. For example, the first session (or sessions, depending on how quickly your children grasp the game) might focus on the 'zip' family. Once 'zip' has been thoroughly learned and digested, the 'zip' Clue Card can be hung on the Word Tree (see p. 14). The Clue Game can then be played for the 'net' family, and so on.

Reinforcing the analogy work

For each word family, supplement the Clue Game analogy work with other analogy activities. Any of the ideas in the Analogy section (p. 99) can be adapted to the rhyme families used in *Supersonic engine juice*. Similarly, any of the Card Games in Sets 3 and 4 can be played, choosing games at an appropriate developmental level.

The children can make their own clue cards for words that rhyme with the Clue Cards 'net', 'zip', 'fan', 'tub', and then hang these on the Word Tree. Ask them to produce a spelling and a small picture icon for their words, just as on the Clue Cards. Each family of words can then be strung together (e.g. on knotted thread) and suspended beneath the appropriate Clue Card, so that all of the shared spelling patterns are clearly visible.

The children can make a wall frieze containing large pictures of a net, a ship, a man, and a tub. They can write rhymes to put into the 'net', to put on the 'ship', to attach to the 'man', and to put into the 'tub'.

Make a flip book for the rime family 'an' (see p. 115). Use the onsets F, M, P, R, T, V, GR. The children can write each word that they can make with the flip book, and illustrate it with a picture.

Make a 'word wheel' for the rime family 'ip' (see p. 116). Use D, H, K, L, N, P, R, S, T, Z. The children can write each word that they can make with the wheel, and then draw a picture of another word that *starts* with the same sound. Alternatively, they can draw the pictures that *start* with the same sound from the Alphabet Frieze, which is easier.

Links with other curriculum areas

'Tub' – washing clothes

Art Make a 3-D display – each child draws, paints, or uses bits of material to create a piece of washing, and pegs it to a washing-line strung across the classroom. Rhyme words can then be stuck to each piece of clothing. Alternatively, make 'wax resist' pictures of scenes from the story. To make a wax resist picture, use crayons to draw the picture first and then paint over the wax with bright coloured paint or dye. If different children paint different scenes, then they can be put into a sequence (*English*) as a display around the room, and as a stimulus for retelling the story (*English*: speaking and listening).

Art/Science Continuing the 'wet' theme, scenes from the story can be painted first in dry powder paint using cotton buds or pieces of sponge, and then in normal wet paint. Which is more effective, wet or dry paint? Which scenes suit dry/wet paint best?

History Discuss the use of tub, scrubbing brush, mangle, etc. in the past and compare with how clothes are washed today.

Science See which clothes take longest to dry once wet, test different materials to see which dry quickest, make it a fair scientific test by cutting pieces of material to the same size. Try different locations to find good places to dry clothes. Put drops of water on bits of cloth stretched over jam jars to test and see which material is most waterproof. Use the results of the test to design clothing for Alex, e.g. a waterproof coat and hat, quick-drying trousers, a warm jumper. Make a collage of Alex using appropriate scraps of materials.

'Fan' – paper fans, blowing

'Can' is also a useful member of this family.

Art Use different kinds of paper to make fans, and create a collage or a mobile of fans. Alternatively, brightly coloured watery paint can be dropped onto paper and children can then use a straw to blow the paint around to create a pattern.

Art Make a 3-D display, using empty, washed drink cans, with rhyming words stuck on them, to make a mobile (also *Maths*: balance). Attach thread to the ring pulls to hang them.

English 'Can' is a useful verb for children to learn, and they enjoy making their own personal book or class book about what they 'can' do, e.g. 'I can speak Urdu', 'I can hop', 'Laura can make a cube out of polydrons', 'Ryan can swim'. A further rhyming 'I spy' book could also be made, with each child drawing a rhyming picture and the wording being 'I can see a . . . '.

Maths/Science Make a collection of cans, e.g. coke cans, food cans (a petrol can is mentioned in the story, but is too dangerous to have in class – make

this a safety talking point). Sort cans by colour, size, shape (they are probably all cylinders – what other things are cylinders?). Look at environmental print on the cans – what words do the children know? (also English). At the end the cans can be sorted and taken for recycling.

Science Hold an Alex vs. McGinty race. Cut out boat shapes from newspaper for each participant in the race. Competitors make their own fans, and when the race starts they use the fan to blow the boats along. Alternative methods of blowing can be investigated, e.g. straws, electric fan, vacuum, foot pump, balloon pump.

'Zip', 'Net', 'Fan' – link via a transport theme (ship, jet, van)

Design Technology Make a margarine tub model ship which floats, or a model van which holds, e.g. four bricks. Alternatively, make a moving two-dimensional van (ship or jet): draw a roadway (sea or sky) onto card. Cut two vertical slits in the card at either end of the roadway (sea or sky) and thread a strip of card through the slits. Draw a van (ship or jet) onto another piece of card, stick it onto the strip, and then move the strip backwards and forwards through the slits to make the van (ship or jet) move along the road (sea or sky).

Maths Data collection, recording, and interpretation. The children can do a survey to find out what sorts of transport members of the class have been on, or who has been on a ship/plane/van. Display the findings on simple Venn diagrams, mappings, and graphs, and get the children to describe the results. Race models of different forms of transport and see whose goes the furthest. Record the results on graphs, etc.

Science How many different ways can you think of to move your van/ship/jet (e.g. push, pull, magnet, electric motor, blow). For a sailing boat, attach a cord and pull it by winding the cord around a pencil/cotton reel. Put the van on a slope.

Alternatively, use balloons to make things go. Make card aeroplanes with a small hole in. The teacher blows up a balloon, sticks the untied end through the hole, and lets go – the plane should take off around the classroom. Or sellotape a straw to the aeroplane and thread the straw on string stretched across the classroom. The teacher blows up the balloon, sticks it to the straw, and lets go – this time the plane moves along the string (i.e. in a straight line). How far does it go, how can we make it go further?

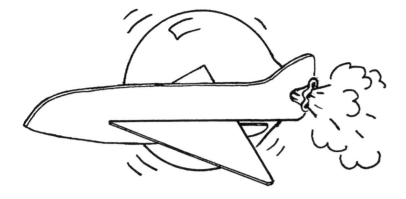

Alternatively, make Alex's jet boat. Take a small plastic bottle with a lid and decorate it to look like the boat. Make a small hole in the bottom. Stick a straw through the hole and seal around the hole with plasticine. Point the straw downwards. Pour some vinegar into the bottle. Wrap some baking soda in a tissue and push it inside the bottle. Quickly put the lid on the bottle and carefully place in a large water tray, with the straw under the water. The baking soda and vinegar mix together to make a lot of gas and foam. You can see the gas coming out of the straw as bubbles, and this makes the boat move along the water.

'Net' – fishing nets

Art Make a display using different sorts of net, e.g. orange/lemon nets from the supermarket, hair nets, fishnet tights, ballet-dancer net (tulle), or fishing net to create the backdrop for a display. Write rhyming words on card fish and attach them to the net as if they have been caught. The children can paint fish, shells, seaweed, etc., and add these to the display.

Rhyme families in Story Rhyme 1

net

get	letter	magnetic
set	petal	alphabet
let	better	Margaret
yet	jetsam	parapet
met	quiet	castanet
wet	market	perpetual
pet	forget	symmetrical
bet	planet	
net	rocket	
fret	magnet	
whet	sunset	
	trumpet	
	comet	
	racket	
	upset	
	ticket	
	puppet	
	velvet	
	target	
	bucket	
	socket	
	Janet	

zip

ship	hippo	slippery
trip	dipper	fingertip
tip	flipper	diplomat
strip	chipmunk	triplicate
slip	tiptoe	inscription
whip	Philip	relationship
skip	tulip	Mississippi
dip	turnip	
hip	parsnip	
lip	gossip	
rip		
grip		
clip		
flip		
chip		
drip		
sip		
zip		
snip		
quip		
nip		
blip		

fan

can	cannot	animal
an	planet	romantic
than	manner	piano
man	sandy	Canada
ran	Santa	banana
plan	panic	candidate
Dan	granny	caravan
pan	flannel	pantomime
Jan	pancake	
fan	canon	
Stan	brandy	
span	pansy	
tan	bandit	
van	manly	
ban	ransack	
bran	began	
scan	Japan	
clan	snowman	
	saucepan	

tub

club	rubber	submarine
rub	public	republic
tub	bubble	substitute
cub	publish	stubbornly
sub	hubbub	publisher
scrub	bathtub	subtraction
shrub	subset	suburban
hub	subway	
grub	rubbish	
stub		
chub		
dub		
snub		
drub		
nub		
pub		

NB Some of the words in the lists may be unfamiliar to the children. However, they have been included so that you can use them later as a basis for extension work.

Scat, cat! focuses the children's attention on the **cat**, **pin**, **bed**, and **dog** rhyme families.

A list of rhyme family words is given on p. 30.

Introducing the Story Rhyme

Begin by reading the story to the children from the Big Book. *Scat, cat!* is about a little mouse who lives in Mrs Moore's house, and who never gets enough crumbs to eat. Mrs Moore's fat dog and cat eat everything in sight, until one day the mouse turns on the cat, and says 'Scat! – enough is enough!'

This is a longer Story Rhyme than *Supersonic engine juice*, and it has a 'fairy tale' feel about it. Use a suitable 'fairy tale' voice! Try and create an atmosphere of magic, wonder, and suspense. For the first reading, make heavy use of the pictures. The pictures have been designed to include rhyming objects (cat, mat, dog, log). Point out some of the rhyming pictures to the children as you read each page. For example, you could say:

Look, here's the cat asleep in her basket, and here's the dog on his mat – the *cat* is near the *mat* . . . and the dog is right near the fire – look, that

log is still burning – the *dog* is by the *log*. They both look fat and happy, don't they – that is a really *fat cat!* I bet they get a lot to eat in Mrs Moore's house . . .

This will help the children to understand the narrative structure of the story, while emphasising the rhymes. For the first reading, concentrate on letting the story build to its climax, introducing the rhyming patterns as a background.

Now read through the story a few more times, but place more emphasis on the rhymes themselves. Help the children to really listen to the rhyming words, to look at them, and to think about why they sound the same. Ask the children guided response questions (see p. 17). Increase the children's listening attention by asking them to show you the rhymes in the pictures that match the rhymes in each verse. Ask them to suggest other rhyming words. Point out the spelling patterns of the rhymes as you read.

Checking narrative comprehension

Talk more generally about the story to check the children's comprehension. Ask them questions like:
- Why was the little mouse looking for crumbs?
- Why did she have to wait until everyone was sleeping?
- Who got all the food in Mrs Moore's house?
- What happened to wake up the dog?
- What happened to wake up the cat?
- What did they do when they saw the little mouse?
- What happened to wake up Mrs Moore?
- Why did the cat get a shock?

You can reinforce the story and the rhyme families by making links with other areas of the curriculum (see ideas at the end of this section).

Links to other ORT stories

If possible, bring in other stories where the 'underdog' carries the day, such as David and Goliath. ORT stories that might be used are: *Floppy the hero, The hedgehog, Kipper's idea, The snowman, Poor old Mum!, It's not fair, Village in the snow, The bully.*

Developing phonological awareness

Use the reinforcement activities suggested in Story Rhyme 1 (p. 18) to consolidate awareness of the phonological patterns in *Scat, cat!* Then develop this awareness with work on onsets, rhymes, and analogies.

Onset work

> **Salient onsets in *Scat, cat!***
> **c   d   m   sc**

The rhyme patterns in *Scat, cat!* do not use onset repetition in the same way as the rhyme patterns in *Supersonic engine juice*. However, the onsets from the most salient words in the story can still be used for work with initial sounds. These are: 'c' (cat), 'd', (dog), 'm' (Mrs Moore and mouse), and 'sc' (Scat!). All of these onsets can be used for oral practice in listening to shared initial sounds.

For example, you could take up the Big Book, and tell the children that you want them to think of words that sound the same at the *beginning* as the names of the characters in the story. Follow the guided response technique used in Story Rhyme 1 (p. 19). For example:

- Read the first page, and then ask them the beginning sound in Mrs Moore's name.
- Ask them if there is someone else in the story whose name begins like Mrs Moore's (the mouse).
- Ask them to tell you some other words that begin with the 'm' sound.
- Point out the mouse on the Alphabet Frieze.
- Ask them what letter they would need to write the 'm' sound.

Do the same for 'cat' and 'dog'. Then move onto the consonant blend 'sc', using similar questions. At this stage, keep the work on this consonant blend at a purely oral level, as its spelling pattern in many English words is SK.

Reinforcing the onset work

This oral work can be supplemented in a number of ways, by adapting the ideas listed in the Onset section (p. 94) to the onsets used in *Scat, cat!* Similarly, any of the Card Games in Set 1 can be played, choosing games at an appropriate developmental level, and the children can use the Alphabet Frieze, the Alphabet

Photocopy Masters, and the Tabletop Alphabets. For example, p. 32 in the Alphabet Photocopy Masters contrasts the onsets 'c', 'd', 'f', and 'n', which have been practised in Story Rhymes 1 and 2.

- The children can make a 3-D collage of objects beginning with the letter C. They could use a carrot, a can, a playing card, a candle, a coin, a toy car . . .
- The children can play an 'add a word' game. Vinnie was *skinny. Skinny* Vinnie went to *sch*ool. *Skinny* Vinnie was *skipping* etc.
- The children can make tongue twisters for D. Derek didn't dawdle. David dances divinely. Doris dashes desperately, daringly, down into a deep dungeon.
- Use the Sound Picture Cards for C, D, and M. Point to each child in turn, and show them one of the cards. Each child has to say a word beginning with the same sound as the word on the card.

Extension work

Extend the oral work to letters:

- The children can add the Letter Card for C to the collage of objects. They can make a label for each object, and write the initial letter for the label in a bright colour.
- The children can write or trace the tongue twisters for D onto long tongues. The children can write the D in each word in a different colour. They can paint pictures of faces for Derek, David, Doris, etc., and display the right tongue coming out of each mouth.
- The children can take it in turns to trace the letters C, D, or M in the air. The others have to say what the letter is, and think of something that begins with that letter. No repeats allowed!
- Sort out the Sound Picture Cards for C, D, and M. Make post-boxes for each letter, putting the correct Letter Card onto the front of each, and ask children to post the pictures into the right boxes. This is a useful assessment activity.
- Put a large C, D, or M onto the classroom door before the children go out to play. As they go out, they have to say a word beginning with the right sound. Change the letter before they come back in.

Obviously, these activities (and others from the Onset section) can be extended to any of the other onsets that attract the children's attention in *Scat, cat!* The children can also play some of the Card Games in Set 3, and trace the relevant Alphabet Photocopy Masters.

Rhyme work

The initial readings of *Scat, cat!* from the Big Book have already focused on rhyme, so you can now extend this informal work. Read the story again with the children, emphasising the rhyming patterns, using the devices of intonation and stress mentioned previously. Ask them if they can remember the rhymes that they thought of for each clue word (*cat, pin, dog, bed*).

Reinforcing the rhyme work

Build on this work by letting the children play the Card Games in Set 2, choosing games at an appropriate developmental level. The rhyme activities in the Story Rhyme Masters can also be used, as most of the activities involve oral rhyme recognition. Supplement this work with some of the ideas in the Rhyme section (p. 97). You can either use general rhyme activities, or adapt them to the rhymes used in *Scat, cat!* For example, for general reinforcement:

- Say and sing some nursery rhymes with the class. Stop before the rhyming words, and ask the children to fill them in. Change some of the rhyming words, and get the children to correct you.

- The children can make up rhyming sentences for their names. Kate was *late*, John has *gone*, Mark is in the *park*, Wendy is *trendy* etc. Children whose names do not have obvious rhymes could make up nonsense rhyming words.

For more specific reinforcement:

- Use the Rhyme Picture Cards from the 'cat', 'pin', and 'dog' families. Sit the children in a circle, and spread the cards face up in the centre. Say a word to each child in turn, and ask them to find a picture that rhymes, e.g. 'My word is 'sat'. Find a picture that rhymes with 'sat''.

- Use the Rhyme Picture Cards from the 'cat', 'pin', and 'dog' families. Sit the children in a circle, and put the shuffled cards in the centre. Each child takes a card in turn, says what it is, and then says a word that rhymes with the picture.

Extension work

Extend the oral work to rime spellings:

- Give the children the Clue Cards for 'cat' and 'dog'. Put two of the Rhyme Picture Cards and two of the Rhyme Word Cards for the two families on the table. Ask the children to sort the Picture Cards into two pairs, one for each Clue Card, and then to put the correct Word Cards next to the pictures.

- The children can paint a picture of Mrs Moore's cat or Mrs Moore's dog. Ask each child for some rhymes, and help them to write the words for their rhymes in big letters. Let them attach the rhymes onto their cats and dogs.

- The children can paint a picture of themselves engaged in their rhyming activity (Mark was in the park). They can write the relevant sentence under each picture, tracing it if necessary, and writing the rhymes in a different colour.

- Choose one of the nursery rhymes for which you changed the rhymes. The children can paint a picture of one of the changed rhymes, and write or trace the new lines underneath (e.g. Hickory Dickory Dock! The mouse fell into a sock! Hickory Dickory Dap! The mouse was wearing a cap!)

Other activities at the end of the Rhyme section also involve spelling patterns, and these can also be adapted to the rhymes in *Scat, cat!* The children can also play some of the Card Games in Set 4, and complete the rhyme activities in the Story Rhyme Photocopy Masters for further consolidation and assessment.

Using analogies

Play the Clue Game using the Clue Cards for 'cat', 'pin', 'bed', 'dog' (see p. 11), playing the game on different days for the different families.

Reinforcing the analogy work

Supplement the Clue Game work for each rhyme family with other analogy activities. Any of the Card Games in Sets 3 and 4 can be played, and any of the ideas in the Analogy section (p. 99) can be adapted to the rhyme families used in *Scat, cat!* For example:

- Give the children the Clue Card for 'pin'. Select the four Rhyme Word Cards for the Clue Card, and one non-rhyme. Ask the children to find all the rhyming words. Repeat for 'cat' and 'dog'. The children should be encouraged to use the shared spelling patterns from the Clue Cards to help them. They can then be encouraged to read the rhymes, and can match the appropriate Rhyme Picture Cards to the Rhyme Word Cards. This is a useful assessment activity. Make the game harder by using four Rhyme Word Cards and three non-rhymes, or by using two different Clue Cards at once.

Make a 'roly rhyme maker' for the 'cat' and 'pin' families. Useful onsets for the 'at' rime are B, C, F, H, M, R, and SC. Useful onsets for the 'in' rime are B, D, F, P, T, CH, and GR. The children can write each word that they make with the roller, and illustrate it with a picture.

Make 'rhyme dice'. Use two cubes. Write the rimes for 'pin', 'cat', and 'dog' on the faces of one cube (each rime can appear twice). Write the onsets B, C, F, H, L, and T on the other. Take the Rhyme Picture Cards which match the words made by the dice and place them face-up on the table (bat, bin, cat, cog, fin, hat, log, tin). The first person to throw each rhyme word on the pair of dice and to read it collects the matching picture card and keeps it. The winner is the person with the most cards at the end.

Links with other curriculum areas

'Cat', 'dog' – pets

Art Make clay animals, and paint them.

Design Technology/Maths Make a model home for a pet, using junk or construction kits (e.g. a basket for a toy dog). Is the home long/wide/high enough for the pet to fit in?

English/PE Look at the way different animals move. What parts of their bodies do they use? Try and move like the animals.

Maths Data collection, recording, and interpretation. The children can do a survey to find out which pets members of the class have at home. Display the findings on Venn diagrams, mappings, or graphs, and get the children to describe the findings to you.

Science What do pets need to live? (e.g. secure, safe home with enough space to move about, food, water, warmth.)

'Pin' – 'pinning' activities

English Play pin the tail on the cat/dog. A group of children can paint a large cat/dog for use in this game. This group work encourages skills of cooperation, planning, speaking, and listening.

Science/English Write onsets and rimes of words on separate cards. Use one colour of card for the onsets and another colour for the rimes. Attach a pin to each card and spread the cards over the floor. Use a magnet suspended on a piece of string to fish for two cards, one of each colour. Put the two cards together to make a word and read the word. Is it a real word or a nonsense word? If it is a real word and the child reads it correctly, then the child keeps the two cards, otherwise the cards are returned to the floor.

'Cat', 'dog' – farms, mice

Drama Play a character game. Choose, say, four characters which make a particular sound (e.g. cat (miaows), dog (barks), mouse (squeaks), Mrs Moore (snores)). Secretly tell each child which character they are going to be (more than one child is the same character). The children can be told their character verbally (in a whisper), by being shown a picture of the character copied from the story book, or by reading the name of the character on a card. When the teacher says 'go', the children mime the characters in order to find each other. Alternatively, they can pretend to be the character by making the appropriate noise. The children have to find all the other children who are the same character and sit together in a group. The winners are the first complete group to sit down.

History Compare farms in the past and present. What sort of farm is depicted in the story book? What would you find on Mr Brown's farm? A fire is used in the story for keeping warm – what ways do we have of keeping our homes warm now?

PE Play some cat and mouse catch games. For example, make some mice line up on one side of the hall. Have two volunteer cats standing on guard in the middle of the hall. The aim is to cross the hall without being caught by a cat. When a mouse is caught the mouse becomes a cat and tries to catch the remaining mice. The mice only run across the hall according to instructions called out by the teacher (e.g. cross the hall if you have white shorts on/ have a brother/ have an 'a' in your name). The winner/winners are the last to be caught.

Alternatively, get the children to stand in a circle. One child is the cat and stands in the centre of the circle. The teacher then calls out the name of the child who is going to be the mouse. The mouse has to run around the outside of the circle, back to his/her original place, before the cat catches him/her. If the mouse is caught, the mouse becomes the cat.

Another variation is to play a mouse-hole game. Place a hoop for every pair of children around the hall. These are the mouse holes, and they can only hold two mice. The mice have to move around the hall according to instructions given by the teacher (e.g. you are going into the kitchen = run; you are passing the cat = tip toe; you are getting onto the table = jumping). When the teacher claps her hands, it means that the cat has woken up and the mice must run into a hole. Any child who is not in a hole, or who is in a hole with more than one other person, is out. The teacher removes a hoop on each go until there are only two mice left, who are the winners.

Design Technology Take two pieces of card, one slightly narrower than the other. Staple a strip of card across the back of the wider card, and fit the narrower card under the strip. Move the narrower card so that it extends then shortens the length of the wider card. Draw a mouse across the cards and move them

so that the mouse will grow longer and then shorter, as it grows in the story book. Alternatively, draw an animal (e.g. a cat) onto card and cut two slits by the eyes. Then get a strip of card with eyes drawn on it to thread through the slits and make the eyes of the animal move.

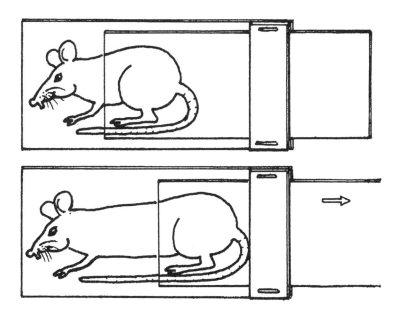

English Listening Skills Play some 'quiet as a mouse' games.

Play Chinese whispers.

Play a game about guessing what's inside a tin by listening – put different objects into tins without the children seeing them.

Get the children to take it in turns to shut their eyes while another child says hello. The first child has to guess the owner of the voice.

Play a 'take the keys' game. The children sit in a circle, with one child in the middle. The child in the middle is blindfolded and has a bunch of keys. The teacher points to a child in the circle who creeps up on the child in the middle and steals the keys. If the child in the middle hears the other child approaching and correctly points at them, then the child must return to the circle.

Play a 'describing' game, using a tray of objects/pictures. One child chooses an object but does not say which one they are thinking about. Other children ask questions to try and discover the object under consideration. The first child can only answer yes or no. Alternatively, one child is shown a simple drawing by the teacher, e.g. a small circle inside a large circle on top of a square. The child describes the drawing to the rest of the class, who have to draw what they think the teacher has drawn.

Rhyme families in Story Rhyme 2

pin

in	into
skin	inside
thin	winter
win	window
tin	dinner
spin	finish
chin	winner
grin	windy
twin	Hindu
gin	begin
fin	robin
bin	basin
din	cabin
kin	Martin
shin	pumpkin
	penguin
	dolphin
	napkin
	margin
	muffin
	toxin

cat

at	matter	natural
sat	atom	attitude
that	attic	satisfy
flat	fatty	batteries
hat	satin	diplomat
fat	hatter	acrobat
bat	tattoo	fanatic
rat	battle	mathematics
pat	rattle	
mat	chatter	
spat	statue	
chat		
scat		
gnat		
vat		
brat		
slat		
tat		

bed

red	bedroom	decided
led	wedding	related
Fred	teddy	excited
fed	medal	medicine
shed	pedal	limited
Ned	edit	beloved
Ed	redden	infrared
sled	noted	edible
Ted	jagged	pedestal
fled	winded	
sped	dogged	
bred		
wed		
bled		
shred		

dog

log	foggy	dogmatic
fog	doghouse	toboggan
frog	foghorn	geography
hog	soggy	photography
smog	goggle	mahogany
bog	bulldog	biography
flog	hedgehog	
jog	bullfrog	
clog		
cog		
grog		
slog		

NB Some of the words in the lists may be unfamiliar to the children. However, they have been included so that you can use them later as a basis for extension work.

The Mungle Flap focuses the children's attention on the **cap**, **hen**, **lid**, and **nut** rhyme families.

A list of rhyme family words is given on p. 38.

Introducing the Story Rhyme

Begin by reading the story to the children from the Big Book. *The Mungle Flap* is about a group of hunters who are off to catch a bird which, in their imaginations, is highly alarming and dangerous. However, for all the brave words of the hunters, they are bungling incompetents, and all of their elaborate traps are simply a device to catch the hen that will lay the eggs for their tea! The adventure is all in their minds.

The Mungle Flap is a humorous story, with a lively rhythm, and has lots of alliteration and rhymes to be emphasised. Try and bring out this liveliness as you read. For example, you could introduce some actions to fit the rhyming words. As you say 'snip, snap', you can make snapping actions with your hands (using your thumb and fingers as a jaw); as you say 'clip, clap', you can clap sharply; as you say 'scrip, scrop, scrap', your voice can rise more and more and your fingers can make clawing actions. The idea is to increase the children's attention level when you say the rhyming words, making them sound exciting. Use intonation to highlight the funny side of the story.

By the second or third reading, encourage the children to chant the repeated parts of the refrain with you as you read it ('So trap, trap, the Mungle Flap')

Then work more slowly through the story, verse by verse. As usual, your goal is to focus the children's attention on the words that rhyme, using guided response questions (see Story Rhyme 1, p. 17).

Checking narrative comprehension

- How did the hunters imagine that the Mungle Flap would look?
- Where did they think the Mungle Flap lived?
- What kind of traps did they make?
- How were the traps supposed to work?
- Were they surprised when they found the Mungle Flap? Why?

You can reinforce the story and the rhyme families by making links with other areas of the curriculum (see ideas at the end of this section).

Links to other ORT stories

You can also talk more generally about how we often imagine something to be more frightening than it really is. This can happen to grown-ups as well as to children!

Some ORT stories you could use are: *At school*, *The dream*, *A monster mistake*.

Developing phonological awareness

Use the reinforcement activities suggested in Story Rhyme 1 (p. 18) to develop awareness of the phonological patterns in *The Mungle Flap*. Then develop this awareness with work on onsets, rhymes, and analogies.

Onset work

Salient onsets in *The Mungle Flap*

fl tr sn cl gl scr

The Mungle Flap makes heavy use of alliteration as well as of rhyme. This Story Rhyme introduces a number of double-consonant onsets and one triple-consonant onset. The most salient onsets are: 'fl' (flap), 'tr' (trap), 'sn' (snip-snap), 'cl' (clip-clap), 'gl' (gloomy glen) and 'scr' (scrip, scrop, scrap!). All of these onsets can be used for oral practice in listening to shared initial sounds.

For example, take up the Big Book, and tell the children that you want them to think of words that sound the same at the beginning as some of the words in the story. Follow the guided response questioning technique given in Story Rhyme 1 (p. 17), for example:

- Ask them the beginning sounds in the Mungle Flap's name.
- Ask them if they can think of someone else whose name begins like Flap (Floppy), and point him out on the Alphabet Frieze.
- Ask them for other words that begin like Flap and Floppy (fly, flower, floor).
- Ask them which letters they would need to write the 'fl' sound.
- Ask the children to separate the two letters orally by exaggerating them ('fff - lll').

Do the same for the other consonant blends.

Reinforcing the onset work

This oral work can then be supplemented in a number of ways. Any of the ideas in the Onset section (p. 94) can be adapted to the onsets used in *The Mungle Flap*, and any of the Card Games in Set 1 can be played. The Alphabet Photocopy Masters (p. 44 focuses on 'fl') and the Tabletop Alphabets provide further opportunities for onset practice.

- The children can make up alliterative sentences about Floppy to practise 'fl'. Floppy was in a flap. Floppy had some flippers. Floppy flew to Finland. Floppy fell down flat etc.

- The children can play an 'add a word' game for 'cl'. Clever Clara clapped her hands. Clever Clara clapped her hands and clasped her clogs. Clever Clara clapped her hands and clasped her clogs because she found a clue in Cleveland, and so on.

- The children can think of more words for the Mungle Flap's 'gloomy glen' to practise 'gl'. Deep in the *gl*oomy *gl*en was a *gl*ow worm, showing a *gl*immer of light. The *gl*oomy *gl*en was *gl*istening with *gl*ue from the hunter's trap.

- Write the onset SCR on a piece of card, and put it on the door of the classroom. As the children pass through the door, they have to say a word with the same onset (scream, screw, scratch, scrip, scrop, scrap).

Extension activities

Extend the oral work to letters. One way of doing this is to play the Clue Game for onsets. Begin with the more able children.

Using the Clue Game for onsets

> Introduce onsets in a separate session of the Clue Game.

The Clue Game is easily adapted to teaching onsets. The game simply focuses on shared onsets rather than on shared rimes. Each word that has a shared onset will have a *different* rime. For some onsets, these different rimes will be familiar from previous Story Rhymes. In such cases, you can ask the children to read the whole word for you, by making an onset analogy and then a rime analogy. This is a good way to begin the Clue Game for onsets.

In other cases, the rime will be unfamiliar, and so the children should only be asked to use their clue to read the *beginning* part of new onset words. Once they become more proficient with the Clue Game, however, you can routinely ask them to read the whole word by making an onset analogy and a rime analogy.

Reading analogies

Begin the game with the clue word 'flap', to teach the onset FL. Make the word up from plastic letters. In cases such as this, there is no Clue Card to use as a guide, and so you can simply spell the word for the children.

> Today we are going to use the Clue Game to work out the *beginnings* of new words. Let's think about words that have the same beginning as 'flap'. I'm going to spell 'flap' for you here, in plastic letters. The letters in 'flap' are F, L, A, P.

Then point out that when you separate the word into its onset and rime, there are *two* letters at the beginning instead of one.

> Look, I'm leaving a gap in my spelling. Why am I doing that? Yes, because there are two parts to 'flap', the 'fl' sound which is spelled with? (children – F, L), and the 'ap' sound which is spelled with? (children – A, P).

> How many letters are there for the beginning part of this word? That's right, there are *two* beginning letters. These two letters always stay together when they make the sound 'fl'. Look, I'm going to make a new word that begins with the letters F, L. Can you read this new word for me?

Put a new word like 'flip' onto the board, also separated into onset and rime. Say something like:

> You can work out how to read the beginning of this new word by using 'flap' as a clue. Which part of 'flap' gives you a clue to this word? That's right, the two letters at the beginning, which are? Yes, F, L. So it's the FL part which gives you a clue, because it's the same in the two words. And F, L at the beginning of a word makes what sound? Yes, 'fl', like in 'flap'.

> So we know the beginning part of the new word. Which part is left over? That's right, the end part. The end of the word has the letters? Yes, I, P. So we need to think of a good clue for the letters I, P. Can you think of a clue from the Word Tree, that has the letters I, P? Let's go and look. That's right, we can use 'zip' as a clue.

Add the Clue Card for 'zip' to the board, and ask the children about the analogy:

> How do we know that 'zip' is a good clue? That's right, because it has the *same* letters at the end. Which letters are at the end of 'zip'? Yes, I, P. What sound do I and P make in 'zip'? That's right, they make an 'ip' sound. So what is the sound at the end of our word? Yes, it must be 'ip' as well.

> So what word do you think that F, L, I, P might spell? Good work! Yes, this new word is 'flip'!

As usual, explicitly model the analogy process for the children, even if they get the new word right. This is good reinforcement.

> Do you know how we tell that this word is 'flip'? We can check with our clues. What does this bit of the word say? (pointing to the onset). It's the same in both words (pointing out the FL in 'flap' and 'flip'). That's right, the letters F,L make the sound 'fl'.

> And what does this bit of the word say? (pointing to the rime). It's the same in both words (pointing out the IP in 'zip' and 'flip'). That's right, the letters I,P make the sound 'ip'.

> So to figure out our new word, we put the two parts together. What are the two parts? Yes, F, L like in 'flap', which makes 'fl', and I, P like in 'zip', which makes 'ip'. So our new word is 'fl – ip', which is 'flip'.

Remember:

> **To read a word that we don't know,**
> **We think of some clues that we *do* know.**

Emphasise that the clues can help with the *beginnings* of words as well as with the ends.

Now use the same procedure with other words that share the same onset. Use 'fl' words that build on previous story rhymes first. These are 'flat' (cat), 'flan' (fan), 'fled' (bed), and 'flog' (dog).

Then add more words to the board with the onset FL. Don't worry if the rime spellings are quite difficult (e.g. fly, flew, fling, Floppy, flower). Just ask the children to read the *beginning* part of each new word by using the clue.

Finish by lining up the plastic letters for each onset on the board, so that you can point out all of the correspondences.

> Yes, flower begins with 'fl', the same as flap, floor begins with 'fl', the same as flap, and fly begins with 'fl', the same as flap. They all have the same sound at the beginning, don't they? Which sound do they share? Yes, 'fl'. So they must all begin with the same letters. Which letters are they? Yes, F - L, making the sound 'f..l'.

Say the sound in an exaggerated way, to emphasise that it consists of two phonemes. The goal is to demonstrate that the beginning sound in words that begin with FL is always predictable from the clue word, even for long words like Floppy or flower.

Partial spelling analogies

Alternatively, ask the children to nominate 'fl' words for you to make. This will help to develop phonological awareness of onsets. Each time, ask them which letters you will need to write the beginning part of the word. This will involve *partial* spelling analogies. Again, the focus is on predictability. If a word sounds like 'flap' at the beginning, it will *always* start with the letters F, L.

Extend the Clue Game to other onsets from the Mungle Flap story. In each case, you should emphasise that all of the words have *two* letters at the beginning (or three, for 'scrip, scrop, scrap'). Always ask the children to tell you the sounds that the pairs or triples of letters make, and say the sound in an exaggerated fashion to emphasise the individual phonemes.

Onsets with familiar rimes

FL	flap flip flan fled flog
CL	clog clip clan club
TR	trap trip
SN	snap snip snub
SCR	scrap scrub scrip
Clue Cards	zip fan tub dog bed cat cap

The Clue Game onset work can be extended by using some of the other onset activities in the Onset section (p. 94):

✎ The children can make a big clown from sugar paper, with CL on his hat. They can paint some pictures of other things beginning with CL, and stick these onto the clown's body (clip, clock, cloud, clog, cliff, clay, clam). They can write or trace the names under each picture, writing the onset in a different colour.

✎ The children can paint some pictures of Floppy undertaking the different activities in their invented sentences (Floppy had some flippers. Floppy flew to Finland). They can write or trace the appropriate sentences under each picture, and use a different colour to write the shared onsets.

✎ The children can make a long train from sugar paper with an engine and coaches, and put a different TR word into each coach (e.g. tree, tray, troll, trap, trunk).

✎ The children can make a book about the onset SCR. They can write a word beginning with SCR on each page, and illustrate the words (e.g. screw, scratch, scruffy, scream, scrape).

✎ The children can make some geometrical 'snowflakes' (see below: Links with other curriculum areas). They can stick them onto a large sheet of sugar paper, and write the word 'snow' at the top. They can write other SN words on/under each flake (e.g. snap, snake, snail, snack).

Other ideas from the Onset section can also be adapted to the onsets in *The Mungle Flap*. The children can also play some of the Card Games in Set 3, and trace over the relevant Alphabet Photocopy Masters.

The Clue Game for onsets: summary checklist

■ Make the clue word at the top of the board.

■ Leave a gap between onset and rime.

Reading

■ Add a new onset word, separated into onset and rime, lining up the spelling pattern of the onset with the clue.

■ Ask the children for the sound of the onset.

Then either

■ Ask the children if they can think of a clue for the rime.

■ Ask them to read the new word for you.

Or

■ Tell them the whole word.

■ Ask them how they can check the beginning sound (they can use analogies).

Spelling

■ Ask the children for a new word to spell.

■ Ask them how to write its onset (they can use the clue word).

■ Ask them how they can check that they are right (they can use analogies).

■ If they think of a word with a familiar rime, ask them how to spell the rime using a Clue Card.

The summary checklist for the Clue Game for Onsets is also provided as a photocopiable resource, see p. 107.

Rhyme work

Read *The Mungle Flap* once again with the children, emphasising the rhyming patterns, using the devices of intonation and stress mentioned previously. Ask them if they can remember the rhymes that they thought of for each clue word (cap, hen, lid, nut).

Reinforcing the rhyme work

Now supplement this initial rhyme work with other rhyming activities. You can adapt the ideas in the Rhyme section (p. 97) to the rhymes used in *The Mungle Flap*. Similarly, any of the Card Games in Set 2 can be played, choosing games at an appropriate developmental level. The rhyme activities in the photocopiable resources can also be used, as many focus on oral recognition of rhyme (coded 'L'). You could also:

- Use the Rhyme Picture Cards for 'hen' and 'cap'. Sit the children in a circle and spread the cards face down in the centre. Children take turns to pick a card and say what the picture is, and something that rhymes with the picture.

- Make pairs of Rhyme Picture Cards out of the 'cat', 'hen', 'pin', 'cap', 'zip', 'fan', and 'dog' families. Each child is given a card, looks at it and then holds it to their chest so that no one else can see it. When the teacher says 'Find your partner', children ask each other 'Do you have a picture which rhymes with . . . ?' The children sit down when they find their partner.

- Use the Rhyme Picture Cards from the 'cat', 'hen', 'pin', 'cap', 'zip', 'fan', and 'dog' families, sorted into rhyming pairs. Make some Bingo boards by placing a selection of one of each pair on blank grids. The remaining cards are placed in a box and players take turns to pick out a card. If players have the picture card on their board which rhymes with the picture on the card that they have chosen, then they put a counter over that picture. The winner is the first to cover all the pictures on their board. An outline of a bingo board is provided as a photocopiable resource, see p. 117.

- Present the children with selections of four Rhyme Picture Cards which rhyme and one card which does not (e.g. men, car, pen, ten, hen). Ask the children to find all the pictures that sound the same and to explain their selection. This is a useful assessment activity.

Extension work

Extend the oral work to rime spellings:

- The children can make a wall frieze of the hunters setting off to hunt for the Mungle Flap. They can make a fierce-looking Mungle Flap for the frieze, and put some of the rhyming words describing the fearsome animal in bright letters around the frieze (snap! clap! scrap!).

- The children can make a large version of the hunters' hut with its iron *grid* and its screw-down *lid*. They can put the rhyming words into the hut (did, rid, kid, hid, bid, skid, grid, slid).

- The children can play the Bingo game described above, but use the matching rhyme words in the box instead of the pictures.

- The children can play the 'find your partner' game described above, but use word cards as well as picture cards. This time the correct partners need a word and a picture (one child's word matches another child's picture). When the teacher says 'Find your partner', the children ask each other 'Do you have a picture/word card that rhymes with . . . ?'

- Present the children with selections of four different Rhyme Picture Cards, and six Rhyme Word Cards, four of which rhyme with the pictures. Ask the children to match the pictures and the words.

You can also use some of the other activities that involve letters suggested in the Rhyme section (p. 97). The children can play some of the Card Games in Set 4, and complete the activities in the Rhyme Photocopy Masters which focus on rime spellings.

Using analogies

Play the rhyming version of the Clue Game using the Clue Cards 'cap', 'hen', 'lid', 'nut'. Play the game on separate days for the different rhyme families.

Reinforcing the analogy work

Supplement the Clue Game work for each rhyme family with other analogy activities. Any of the Card Games in Sets 3 and 4 can be played, and any of the ideas in the Analogy section (p. 99) can be adapted to *The Mungle Flap* rhyme families.

Make a 'flip' book for the 'cap' family. Write the rime spelling pattern on the last page of the book, and the onsets G, L, M, T, FL, CL, SN, and SCR on shorter pages in front. Ask the children to flip the pages, naming each rhyming word as they do so. If they forget the words, they can add a small picture as a memory aid under each flap.

Make a simple jigsaw for each of the four rhyming families. To make one jigsaw, put a Clue Card onto the centre of a big piece of card. Now write some family words in the spaces around the Clue Card, and draw irregular jagged shapes around each family word. Cut the pieces out, and jumble them together. Ask the children to make up the jigsaw. A jigsaw outline is also provided as a photocopiable resource (p. 122), and can be enlarged on the copier.

The children can complete two jigsaws at once, mixing the pieces from both jigsaws together. They can extend this to three clue jigsaws, or even to all four.

Use a selection of Rhyme Word Cards from the 'cap' and 'hen' families. Spread the cards face-down in front of the children. Children take turns to pick a card and to read the word on it. They then have to think of a word which rhymes with the word on the card, and try to spell it on a wipe board. They should be encouraged to use the spelling pattern of the rhyme word on the card that they have chosen to help them.

Links with other curriculum areas

'Cap' and family

Art **tap** Make a 3-D display. Make 'teardrops' out of card, and write a rhyme family word on each drop. Make an outline of a tap, and use to create a mobile.

Design Technology **trap** Make a trap or a Mungle hut to catch/hold the Mungle Flap, using junk or construction kits. Include grids, locks, and the other features mentioned in the Story Rhyme. Write rhyming words on cards and suspend these inside the models, or attach with Blu-tack to the outside of the models.

Geography **map** Make a map showing all the geographical features mentioned in the story (e.g. fen, Mungle Flap's den). Further map work can be related to the children's own experiences (e.g. map of how get to school/the hall from the classroom/plan of my bedroom).

Alternatively, if squared paper or sticky squares are used to mark the locations on the story map, then it could double as a base board for a dice game. Before being allowed to have a go, the child could have to say/read a pair of rhyming words.

Alternatively, make a 3-D map in a sand-tray, using papier mâché over junk boxes or construction kits.

Geography/Information Technology A large map can be made and a roamer or a turtle can be decorated to represent the hunters. The children can programme the roamer or turtle to move around the map looking for the Mungle Flap (and once again, a game can be created).

Maths Make a collection of caps and sort them according to colour/material/size etc. Compare warm-/cold-weather caps. Measure the children's heads using strips of paper and order the strips according to length.

PE Create a Mungle Flap game. Draw four pictures of places from the story book, e.g. the glen, the fen, the Mungle Flap's den, and the hut (or make a collage, using natural materials such as leaves, grasses, wood bark). Write the location words on cards (e.g. glen, fen, den, hut). Place one picture in each of four corners of the hall and the cards in a box. Children move around the hall pretending to be hunters or Mungle Flaps. When the teacher claps her hands (or turns off the music if used) the children must go to one of the four places. Children then take turns to remove a card from the box without looking and read the word. All the children at that place are out. The card is returned to the box. Winners are the last few to be out.

Science Make a Mungle Flap appear in a trap. Take a small piece of card and draw a Mungle Flap in the middle of one side and a Mungle Flap trap in the middle of the other side. Sellotape the card to the top of a pencil. Roll the pencil quickly in your hands and look at the card. It looks as if the mungle trap has been caught and is inside the trap!

'Hen' – Mungle Flap/hen

Art Make a hen. Cut an outline out of card and decorate the body shape. Make a fan out of paper and thread through a slit in the body. Open out the fan as the wings of the bird.

Design Technology Make a hen that moves. Cut an outline out of card and decorate the body. Cut out two large wings and attach them to the body with sellotape such that the sellotape forms a hinge and the wings can move up and down. Fix a long thread from the centre of one wing to the centre of the other wing. Hang from the mid-point of the thread and pull the body down. The bird will flap up and down.

Alternatively, make a Mungle Flap with jaws that 'snip snap'. Cut out the body shape from card, minus the lower jaw, and decorate. Attach the lower jaw to the mouth with a butterfly clip. Use a strip of card joined to the end of the lower jaw but hidden behind the Mungle Flap to act as the handle on the scissor action which opens and shuts the jaw. (Eyes that glow red could be added using a simple electric circuit and red cellophane.)

Design Technology/English Make a 'flap' book about a hunt for something, e.g. the Mungle Flap. The flaps could be bushes and each one could conceal a rhyming object for the hunters to find (drawn by the children and with the word written by it). The Mungle Flap should only be found at the very end of the story.

English Use information books to discover where different birds make their nests. Why are they in certain places (e.g. safety, food)? Stress that we must not disturb/touch nests.

Alternatively, have an egg hunt. Decorate egg shapes on one side and write a rhyming word on the other. Use a set of rhyming words for each pair of children. Children work in pairs to find a set of say four eggs that rhyme, replacing eggs that do not rhyme with the set that they are collecting for others to find.

Maths Make a collection of feathers and sort/count them. Use them in a collage of the Mungle Flap. Count how many eggs a Mungle Flap would lay in a week. What about if there were two Mungle Flaps?

Music The children can retell the story using sounds. Body sounds can be used to accompany the Mungle Flap description, the hunters journey (e.g. rubbing hands could represent walking through grass, slapping thighs could represent running), and so on. Instruments that 'clip clap' like the wings could be investigated, and different beaters tried.

Science/Maths Use eggs in cooking. Consider the shape of the eggs (roll in a circle, not roll away), and how they change when heated.

'Nut'

Science Make a collection of nuts and look at them through magnifying glasses. Use information books to identify them. **NB** Remember that some children are highly allergic to nuts, and be aware of the dangers of choking on nuts. It is best not to eat any.

Maths **cut** Carry out some cutting investigations. Take a long piece of string and cut it in half. How many pieces will you get – predict then count. Hold the pieces together and cut in half again. How many pieces will you get – predict then count. Keep cutting the pieces in half and predicting and counting the new number of pieces. Can you see a pattern in the number of pieces you get?

Alternatively, do a shape investigation. Cut out different paper shapes (such as square, oblong, equilateral triangle, circle, hexagon). Cut several of each shape. Choose one shape. How many ways can you cut your shape in half? Try another shape. Display your findings by using the half shapes to make a pattern and stick them on card.

Rhyme families in story rhyme 3

cap

map	happy	capital
flap	apple	unhappy
trap	captain	rapidly
tap	happen	pineapple
lap	rapid	happier
clap	napkin	tapestry
wrap	scrapbook	apparatus
snap	kidnap	
gap	unwrap	
sap		
scrap		
strap		
slap		
nap		
chap		
rap		
yap		
pap		

hen

when	engine	energy
then	enjoy	general
men	pencil	enemy
ten	twenty	invention
Ben	penny	adventure
pen	entry	suddenly
den	tennis	carpenter
glen	Wendy	evenly
wren	dentist	
ken	even	
yen	often	
	children	
	given	
	happen	
	kitten	
	listen	
	open	
	seven	
	garden	
	taken	

lid

did	middle	consider
rid	hidden	idiot
hid	kidnap	timidly
kid	riddle	invalid
slid	stupid	rapidly
bid	undid	pyramid
grid	solid	video
squid	David	solidly
skid	horrid	considerate
mid	timid	
quid	ridden	

nut

but	butter
cut	button
shut	nutmeg
hut	putty
glut	gutter
smut	shutter
gut	peanut
rut	haircut
tut	coconut
strut	
jut	

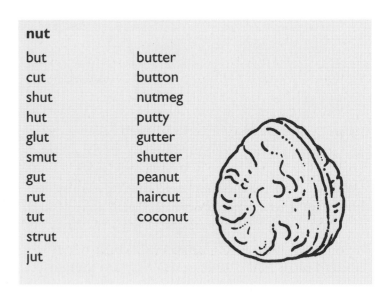

NB Some of the words in the lists may be unfamiliar to the children. However, they have been included so that you can use them later as a basis for extension work.

> *Bad day, good day* focuses the children's attention on the **sad**, **hit**, **leg**, and **sun** rhyme families.
>
> A list of rhyme family words is given on p. 44.

Introducing the Story Rhyme

As usual, begin with the Big Book. *Bad day, good day* is a story about a little girl's feelings – she has a bad week, but then there is a great turn-around at the end when she has a wonderful party for her birthday. In fact, the little girl is really quite naughty and wild, and so her bad week is partly the result of her own bad behaviour!

The rhymes in *Bad day, good day* are not at the end of each line, but are at points in each sentence that are highlighted by *rhythm*. Make sure that you emphasise the rhythm in each verse to bring out the sounds of the rhymes.

Some of the events and feelings in the story are shown via the little girl's speech/thought bubbles, which always contain a rhyme family word. Point these out to the children as you read.

As you read through the Story Rhyme again, ask the children to supply certain of the key rhyme family words. For example, in the first verse you could ask them to supply 'lad', and the second 'bad'. Focus attention on the *spellings* of the family words by pointing to the key words in the speech/thought bubbles, and encouraging the children to tell you what they say. Do the same with key words in the text. Move on to an exclusive focus on the sounds of the family words, using guided response questions (see Story Rhyme 1, p. 17).

Checking narrative comprehension

- What happened to the little girl on Monday?
- Was Joe being naughty on purpose?
- What happened to the little girl on Tuesday?
- Did she mean to lose her temper?
- What happened to the little girl on Wednesday?
- Did she mind having to miss PE?

and so on.

You can reinforce the story and the rhyme families by making links with other areas of the curriculum (see ideas at the end of this section).

Links to other ORT stories

If you like, bring in other stories about naughty little girls or boys (*My naughty little sister, Pippi Longstocking*). Some ORT stories you could use are: *New trainers, The baby-sitter, The water fight, The snowman, Adam's car*.

Developing phonological awareness

Use the reinforcement activities suggested in Story Rhyme 1 (p. 18) to consolidate awareness of the phonological patterns in *Bad day, good day*. Then develop this awareness with work on onsets, rhymes, and analogies.

Onset work

> Salient onsets linked to *Bad day, good day*
>
> **h l s**

The rhyming pattern of *Bad day, good day* does not draw the children's attention to any particular onsets. Nevertheless, you can still use the Story Rhyme as a basis for onset work, as the Clue Cards can be used for onset work as well as for rhyme work.

The Clue Cards for the rhyme families in Story Rhyme 4 have some useful onsets ('h' - hit, 'l' - leg, and 's' - sun and sad). The onset H is on the Clue Card 'hen' (Story Rhyme 3), and the onset L is on the Clue Card 'lid' (Story Rhyme 3). This provides an opportunity for consolidation and reinforcement, as you can use these Clue Cards to stress the shared beginning sounds of the clue words 'sad', 'hit', 'leg' and 'sun'.

For example, to practise the onset H, you can:

■ Display the Clue Card for 'hit'.

■ Ask the children if they can see any words on the Word Tree that begin with the same sound as 'hit', and introduce 'hen' as an example.

■ Ask the children to listen out for other words in the story that begin with the same sound as 'hit' and 'hen'.

■ Ask them whether they can see any pictures in the story whose names begin with the same sound as 'hit' and 'hen'.

■ Ask them which word on the Alphabet Frieze begins with the same sound as 'hit' and 'hen', and which letter they need to write this sound.

■ Ask the children to think of other words that sound the same at the beginning as 'hit' and 'hen'.

There are quite a few words in the story that begin with 'h', but some of them are verbs and adjectives rather than nouns (have, had, hate, horrid). This might make them more difficult to spot. Encourage the children to keep thinking as this will be good listening practice for them.

Reinforcing the onset work

You can now supplement this work in a number of ways. As usual, the Alphabet Frieze, Alphabet Photocopy Masters, Tabletop Alphabets, and Card Games (Set 1) all provide support activities. There are also lots of ideas in the Onset section (p. 94), which can be adapted to the onsets in *Good day, bad day*. For example:

◖ The children can think of a number of adjectives for 'h' to describe the little girl's day (happy day, horrid day, helpful day, hot day, heavenly day).

◖ The children can play an 'add a word' game for 'l', describing a good or bad day that they might have had (I had a good day because the weather was *lovely*, I had a good day because I had a nice *lunch*.

◖ The children can make up alliterative sentences for 's' (on a sunny summer Saturday Sally started singing a song about the sea).

Extension work

Extend this oral work to letters:

The children can make pictures of the kind of day that the little girl had (hot day, helpful day). They can write or trace a sentence describing her day underneath each picture, writing the onset H in a different colour.

The children can make a wall frieze for the sentence 'I had a good day because . . . ', in which they each paint a picture of themselves experiencing the activity that they suggested for L. The different reasons for their good days can be written onto strips of paper, with the onset L picked out in a different colour in each sentence.

Take the Letter Cards for H, L, and S. Show each child one of the letters at random. The children have to say a word that begins with the sound of the letter. They aren't allowed to repeat any words.

Pick out the Sound Picture Cards for H, L, and S. Take the corresponding letter cards, and ask the children to sort the picture cards into four groups, one for each letter. This is a useful assessment exercise.

Again, any of the other activities in the Onset section (p. 94) can be adapted to these onsets, and the Alphabet Photocopy Masters provide further scope for consolidation and assessment. The children can also play some of the Card Games in Set 3.

Rhyme work

Bad day, good day has a very simple rhythmic structure that can be used as a basis for further work on rhyme. Begin by reading through the Story Rhyme again from the Big Book, asking the children to pick out the rhymes. Then reinforce the rhyming work by changing the different verses in amusing ways. For example, you can use the children's own names, and use incidents from their own lives.

Monday was a bad day,
Tom's a naughty lad – day

You may prefer to make up verses emphasising lots of *good* things that have happened to the children!

Monday was a good day,
We all did as we should – day

The idea of simple rhyming verses could then be extended to focus on the family words, changing the verse pattern if necessary.

Monday was the day of dad,
this day for dad was really bad.
He went to work and he got mad.
When he got home he felt quite sad.

Reinforcing the rhyme work

You can build on this work by supplementing it with some of the ideas in the Rhyme section (p. 97). Any of the Card Games in Set 2 can be played, choosing games at an appropriate developmental level, and the rhyme activities in the Story Rhyme Photocopy Masters can also be used (sheets coded 'L' are based on oral recognition of rhyme).

Another way to reinforce the oral rhyming work is to continue with the 'silly poem' theme, either by adapting it to the support materials like the Rhyme Picture Cards, or by taking the children's own poems further:

- The children can mime to their own verse of the adapted story. For example, Tom can mime forgetting his PE kit and missing games.
- Use the Rhyme Picture Cards for 'sun' ('bun', 'run', 'nun'). The children have to invent a poem that uses some of these pictures. It doesn't matter if the poems are extremely simple ('I sat in the sun, and ate a bun'), the act of producing a poem will still have a beneficial effect. You can extend this poetry game to other Rhyme Picture Cards as well. Alternatively, you can give the children a rhyme family word to make a two-line poem around ('I saw my dad, and I felt glad').
- The children can use puppets to retell the events in the Story Rhyme. They could do a puppet show to the Story Rhyme Tape, or they could each memorise a verse of the story and then recite it as the puppets create the action.

Extension work

As usual, this involves linking the oral work to rime spellings.

- Each child can write out their two-line poem in their best writing, and then illustrate it. The poems can form a wall display, grouped by rhyme family.
- The children can make class books describing the events of the different days of the week, or books of the different poems that were generated earlier. Groups of children could each produce a different book, making a picture for each line, and writing the text underneath. Thus the poem for the 'Monday' book would have different pictures for the lines 'Monday was a good – day' and 'We all did as we should – day'. If the words in the poems happen to have different rime spellings (as in good–should), make this a teaching point.

Other activities at the end of the Rhyme section also involve spelling patterns, and these can also be adapted to the rhymes in *Bad day, good day*. The children can play some of the Card Games in Set 4, and use the Story Rhyme Photocopy Masters for further consolidation and assessment (sheets coded 'RW' involve writing rimes).

Using analogies

Play the rhyming version of the Clue Game for the Clue Cards 'dad', 'hit', 'leg', and 'sun', playing the game on different days for each different family.

Reinforcing the analogy work

Supplement the Clue Game with other Analogy activities from the Analogy section (p. 99), adapting them to the rime families in *Bad day, good day*. The Card Games provide further opportunities for consolidation.

- Copy out different verses of the Story Rhyme, leaving gaps for the rhyme family words. The children have to write the correct words in the gaps, using the Clue Cards and the Alphabet Frieze to help them.
- Ask the children to do a word search for either 'hit', 'sad', or 'sun'. Let them choose some other stories or some old magazines as a basis for their search. Their task is to find all the words in these stories that are spelled with the same rime as their clue word, and to copy them out. Then see how many they can read for you, using the Clue Card and the Alphabet Frieze to help them. Alternatively, the children can fill in the word search grid on p. 123 or in the Story Rhyme Photocopy Masters and give them to each other to do. As the 'hit' family has 206 members, the 'sad' family 165, and the 'sun' family 341, they should be able to find a few rhymes in any story book or magazine.
- Play some of the 'Bun Shop' games described below.

Links with other curriculum areas

'Leg'

Design Technology/Art Draw a person (e.g. a character from a story book) minus the legs on a piece of rectangular card. The body should end at the edge of the card. Cut a circle out of card with a diameter just less than the width of the rectangle. Draw legs radiating out of the centre of the circle, looking as though they are running. Put a butterfly clip through the centre of the circle and attach it to the mid-point of the person's body, pinning it to the edge of the rectangle so that half of the circle hangs down below the card. Spin the card quickly to give the effect of running.

Design Technology/Art/Maths Make models out of clay, dough, or plasticine of animals with no/two/four legs and sort into sets. Make card versions and use butterfly clips to make the legs move.

'Knit'

Design Technology Make pompoms: wrap wool around two card circles with a hole in the centre. Cut the wool round the edge of the circles, and wind a piece of wool between the cards. Pull off the card circles, and fluff out the pompoms. Add decoration such as card eyes or pipe cleaner legs to make a pompom person or animal.

Maths/Science Make a collection of knitted scraps or old garments and look at them through a microscope. Can you see how they are made? Look at the labels on the garments to see what they are made of. Take pieces the same size and see what happens when you wash them and leave them to dry.

Science Collect different types of wool. Test the strength of the wool by tying equal lengths of wool to a bar and tying on weights.

'Sun' – also 'bun', 'run'

Art For a display, make a large sun by folding a piece of gold or yellow paper into a fan. Cut the ends to a point and staple the fan together in the middle. Open out the two sides to form a circular shape. The children can make their own little versions. Alternatively, a weather mobile with sun, clouds, rainbow and rhyme words written on the clouds can be made.

English What would you take with you on holiday to a hot country? What would you like/dislike about being somewhere hot? Draw what you would take in your suitcase and stick the pictures to a piece of paper cut to the shape of a case with a handle attached.

Maths **bun** Sing and act out 'Five currant buns in the baker's shop'. Make buns from painted rolled up paper and create a baker's shop. Use the shop to answer mathematical questions: there are 6 buns and Sarah buys 2, how many are left? There are 2 buns on this tray and 3 buns on this tray, how many altogether? If there are five buns and I want ten how many more will the baker have to make? If there are 10 buns and you share them out between James and Farian, how many will they each have?

Create a game based on the bun shop. For example: use two dice marked 1 to 3. The children take turns to throw the dice and to add/find the difference between/multiply the resulting numbers together. They then take that many buns. The winner is the first child to get ten buns.

Alternatively, use two dice, one with onsets written on the faces (e.g, s, r, b, f, n, p) and the other with rimes (e.g., un, it, ad, each written twice). The children take it in turns to throw the die and put them together. If they read the word correctly, they can take a bun. The winner is the first to get ten buns.

Alternatively, write sets of rhyming words on cards, one word on each card. The children take it in turns to take and read a card, to provide another rhyming word, or to write another rhyming word. If they are correct they get a bun. The winner is the first to get ten buns.

PE **run** Investigate different ways of moving (e.g. running, skipping, hopping, jumping). The children sit in a circle and the teacher goes round numbering the children 1 to 4. Then the teacher tells the children a way of moving, e.g. running, and calls a number. All the children who have been given that number then move round the outside of the circle back to their places in the way described by the teacher.

Alternatively, the children can move around the room but when the teacher claps her hands they must move in a different way. Extend this by having the children work in pairs and take it in turns to copy one another. Get them to describe how their partner is moving.

Science How should we protect ourselves on a sunny day? Design a good sun hat. Alternatively, put different-coloured pieces of paper in a sunny place. To make a fair test, place identical pieces somewhere out of the sun. What happens to the paper? Use this effect to create a picture. Cut out shapes or use stencils. Arrange them on a piece of coloured paper, then leave it in the sun. After a couple of weeks, remove the shapes and stencils.

Science/Geography Observe and record the weather on a chart. Make a weather wheel by cutting out a circle and drawing lines across it to form quarters. In each quarter draw a different sort of weather, towards the edge of the circle. Make a card pointer and attach it to the centre of the circle with a butterfly clip. Move the pointer so that it points to the correct weather condition.

'Day'

Although it is not a rhyme family word here, the theme 'day' runs through this Story Rhyme, and provides an obvious basis for links with other curriculum areas. It is also a word for the 'hay' family used in Story Rhyme 5, so some of these activities could be used in conjuction with that Story Rhyme instead.

Art/Maths Look at pieces of wrapping paper and discuss how the pattern is created (usually it is a repeated pattern). The children can then make their own wrapping paper by printing with cut potatoes, everyday objects such a bottle lids or leaves, sponges, a polystyrene food container with a design incised on it by drawing on it with a pencil, a piece of card with string stuck on it in an interesting design, etc.

Design Technology Design a lunchbox. How big should it be? What should it be made out of? What shape should it be?

English Write about or draw pictures of your own good/bad day. What makes us feel good/bad? How can we help to make others feel good? Create drawings of people with happy/sad faces and thought bubbles showing in pictures and writing what makes them happy or sad. NB this activity can also be linked to the nonsense verses created in the rhyme activities.

Alternatively, make a collection of words that describe how we are feeling and sort them into good and bad feelings. These could be displayed in two thought bubbles. Write the words on cards, e.g. happy, angry, excited, mad, sad. Let the children take it in turns to pick a card, read the word on it (with help if necessary), and mime that emotion. The others have to guess what is written on the card.

Maths Data collection, recording, and interpretation. Help the children to do a survey of class birthdays. Display the findings on Venn diagrams, mappings, and graphs, and get children to describe the results.

Alternatively, use the children's lunchboxes as a basis for this activity (the little girl dropped her lunch on Thursday). The children can do a survey to find out who has a packed lunch and what people have in their lunch boxes. Display the findings on Venn diagrams, mappings, graphs, and get children to describe the results.

Maths/English Make a class book describing what happens on each day of the week.

Science/English Create a feely box covered with birthday wrapping paper. The teacher secretly places objects in a box with holes cut in the side. On someone's birthday, the children take it in turns to feel in the box and guess what is hidden in the birthday box.

Alternatively, the children can describe what they can feel while the others try and guess, write, or draw what is in the box.

Alternatively, use 3-D shapes for the birthday box (or the Monday box). The children take turns to feel and guess what shape is hidden in the box. Or they can describe what they can feel while others try and guess what the shape is.

Rhyme families in Story Rhyme 4

sad

had	shadow	admiral
bad	saddle	radical
glad	badly	gradual
dad	ladder	graduate
mad	daddy	adhesive
lad	madam	advertise
pad	tadpole	badminton
clad	madly	addition
cad	sadden	
fad	gladly	
shad		
brad		
gad		

leg

beg	beggar	regular
peg	nutmeg	negligent
Meg	bootleg	Gregory
keg	pregnant	
dregs		

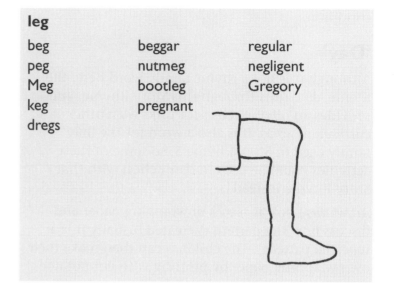

hit

it	little	Italy
bit	city	benefit
sit	British	citizen
fit	kitten	inherit
split	pity	pitiful
lit	litter	inhabit
kit	unit	revisit
pit	visit	inhibit
quit	digit	critical
slit	rabbit	bitterly
wit	limit	
knit	exit	
spit	bandit	
skit		
writ		
grit		

sun

run	under	understand
fun	until	unhappy
gun	hundred	abundant
spun	running	uneven
shun	funny	sunflower
dun	sunlight	uncommon
nun	thunder	uncover
pun	tunnel	
bun	bundle	
stun	bunny	
	punish	
	undo	
	begun	
	outrun	
	shotgun	
	uncle	
	hungry	
	jungle	
	fungus	

NB Some of the words in the lists may be unfamiliar to the children. However, they have been included so that you can use them later as a basis for extension work.

Who wants to play with a troll? focuses the children's attention on the **jam**, **wig**, **shop**, and **hay** rhyme families.

A list of rhyme family words is given on p. 49.

Introducing the Story Rhyme

Begin by reading the children the Big Book. *Who wants to play with a troll?* is a slightly zany story about Little Troll who can't find anyone to play with her – all of the 'adult' trolls (called Grondles) are far too busy doing weird and wonderful things. In the end Little Troll runs away to see if the human children will play with her. The story has a happy ending – the children invite her to their party.

The rhyming pattern in *Who wants to play with a troll?* is easy to follow, and the verse structure has a strong rhythm, which should be brought out as you read. However, there are also embedded rhymes in the middle of lines, and you can encourage children to listen out for these on repeated readings (e.g. in the second verse we have *Stay* and *play* . . . I must *pop* to the *shop*).

On repeated readings, encourage the children to supply the name of each Grondle, and the name of the rhyming activity (e.g. in the first verse the children would say *Gram* and *jam*). As usual, final readings should focus the children's attention on the rhyme family words, using guided response questions (see Story Rhyme 1, p. 17).

Checking narrative comprehension

- Why couldn't Grondle Gram play with Little Troll?
- What was Grondle Gram using to make jam? Would that jam taste good? Might it make you ill?
- Why couldn't Grondle Gree play with Little Troll?
- How big do you think dragon's eggs are? What do baby dragons look like?
- Why couldn't Grondle Grig play with Little Troll?

You can also reinforce the story and the rhyme families by making links with other areas of the curriculum (see ideas at the end of this section).

Links to other ORT stories

You could read stories to the children focusing on play. ORT stories that could be used are: *The toys' party*, *Nobody wanted to play*, and *Come in*.

Developing phonological awareness

Use the reinforcement activities suggested in Story Rhyme 1 (p. 17) to consolidate awareness of the phonological patterns in *Who wants to play with a troll?* Then develop this awareness with work on onsets, rhymes, and analogies.

Onset work

Salient onsets in *Who wants to play with a troll?*

gr tr sh j w h

The rhyming pattern of *Who wants to play with a troll?* emphasises the double-consonant onset 'gr', as the Grondle Trolls have names that begin with 'gr'. Another salient onset is 'tr', as the children's sympathies will be drawn to Little Troll. As in Story Rhyme 4, the Clue Cards also provide a useful basis for onset work. The Clue Cards for 'hen' (Story Rhyme 3) and for 'hit' (Story Rhyme 4) use the same onset as for 'hay' but 'j' (jam) and 'w' (wig) are new. The Clue Card for 'shop' enables the introduction of the onset 'sh'. Emphasise the teaching point that 'sh' has two letters, but only one sound.

Use the Clue Cards to teach these onsets in the ways suggested in Story Rhyme 4 (p. 39). You can use the story and the pictures as a source of other words with shared onsets. You can also use the Alphabet Frieze, which includes the onsets 'gr' (Gran) and 'sh' (shoe).

Reinforcing the onset work

This oral work can be supplemented by adapting the ideas listed in the Onset section (p. 94) to the onsets used in *Who wants to play with a troll?* Similarly, any of the Card Games in Set 1 can be played, choosing games at an appropriate developmental level, and the children can use the Alphabet Frieze, the Tabletop Alphabets, and the Alphabet Photocopy Masters (see p. 42 for 'sh', and p.43 for 'tr').

- The children can make up some tongue twisters about Grondles (a great, big, greasy, grimy, grotty, grinning Grondle).
- The children can think of some adjectives to describe trolls (a tricky troll, a truthful troll, a trendy troll, a truly tremendous troll etc.).
- The children can describe the things you can find in the Grondle Shop, which all begin with 'sh' (a shark fin, a shelf-full of dragons eggs, a shiny bat cage etc.).

Extension work

Extend the oral work letters.

- The children can write or trace the tongue twisters about the Grondles onto long tongues, using a different colour to emphasise the onset GR. They can paint some Grondle heads, and display the tongues coming out of their mouths.
- The children can make a wall frieze of the Grondle Shop, using collage. They can label the different items for sale, marking the onset SH in a different colour for each item. Alternatively, they can make a real shop in the classroom (see Links with other curriculum areas).
- Take the Sound Picture Cards for W, J, SH, and TR, and add a few mismatches (such as the Sound Picture Cards for C and P). Pick out the Letter Cards for W, J, SH, and TR, and ask the children to match the pictures to the right letters. Tell them that they won't all match!

You can also play the Clue Game for Onsets for the onsets SH, GR, and H (see Story Rhyme 3, p. 31):

Onsets with familiar rimes
SH ship shed shin shut shun
TR trip trap tram tray
GR gran grip grub grin grog grid grit
Clue Cards zip fan tub pin bed dog lid cap nut hit sun day jam

As usual, other activities from the Onset section can also be extended to the onsets in *Who wants to play with a troll?* The children can play some of the Card Games in Set 3, and trace the relevant Alphabet Photocopy Masters.

Rhyme work

Begin by reading *Who wants to play with a troll?* once more, asking the children to pick out the rhymes for you. As in Story Rhyme 4, you could then experiment with changing some of the verses in amusing ways, thinking up new excuses for the Grondles to avoid playing with Little Troll. For example:

'I'm bored today', said Little Troll.
'Can't play', said Grondle Grig.
'I've got to put the bats back in
and teach the pig a jig'.

Reinforcing the rhyme work

You can supplement this work with some of the ideas in the Rhyme section (p. 97), adapting them to the rhymes used in *Who wants to play with a troll?* Any of the Card Games in Set 2 can be played, choosing games at an appropriate developmental level, and a couple of the rhyme activities in the Story Rhyme Photocopy Masters can also be used (sheets coded 'L' focus on oral recognition of rhyme). Again, an obvious way to reinforce the oral rhyming work is to continue to think up rhyming activities based on Grondles.

- The children can invent some more Grondles, and decide what their rhyming activities would be (e.g. Grondle Grub, likes to scrub; Grondle Grin, likes to win; Grondle Grad, he's quite bad!).
- The children can change the Grondle Shop so that it only sells rhyming things. They can take it in turns to invent new rhymes. 'I went to the Grondle Shop and I bought some jam.' 'I went to the Grondle Shop and I bought some ham.' or 'I went to the Grondle Shop and I bought some hay/clay.'

The children can find some more animals for Grondle Grig to look after. Each group of animals can have a rhyming skill: Grondle Grig's bats, all chase cats! Grondle Grig's pigs, all dance jigs! Grondle Grig's frogs, all jump logs! Grondle Grig's bears, all eat pears!

Extension work

Link the oral work to rime spellings:

The children can paint a picture of their Grondle, and write his or her name and favoured activity beneath it: Grondle Grin, likes to win!

The children can add pictures of the rhyming items to the wall frieze of the Grondle Shop, or to the real shop in the classroom. For example, they can add some jam and some ham, with their labels.

The children can create a wall frieze of Grondle Grig's zoo. They can depict his frogs jumping logs, his pigs dancing jigs, and so on. They can make signposts for the visitors to the zoo, advertising each activity: Pigs dancing jigs! Frogs jumping logs!

Any of the other activities in the Rhyme section that use spelling can also be adapted to the rhymes in *Who wants to play with a troll?* The children can play some of the Card Games in Set 4, and use the rest of the activities in the Story Rhyme Photocopy Masters, which focus on writing rimes (coded 'RW'), for further consolidation and assessment.

Using analogies

Play the rhyming version of the Clue Game for the Clue Cards 'jam', 'wig', 'shop', and 'hay'. Play the game on different days for each family.

Reinforcing the analogy work

Supplement the Clue Game work for each rhyme family with other analogy activities. Any of the Card Games in Sets 3 and 4 can be played, and any of the ideas in the Analogy section (p. 99) can be adapted to the rhyme families used in *Who wants to play with a troll?*

If the children enjoyed the word-search activity used in Story Rhyme 4, repeat it for 'jam' (197 rhymes), 'shop' (136 rhymes), and 'hay' (148 rhymes).

The children can create some new Clue Cards for the rhyme families in the story. They will need to

print the rhyming word in big letters, and draw a picture icon. Good illustrable rhymes include 'pig', 'dig', 'twig', 'ham',' tram', 'mop', 'top' (spinning variety), and 'tray'. They can hang the new Clue Cards onto the Word Tree, if possible suspending them from the original Clue Card to emphasise the shared rimes.

Extension work with longer words

One simple way to extend the analogy work for any Story Rhyme is to use analogies for words of more than one syllable (see also p. 18, Story Rhyme 1). To work out how to read these longer words, the children will need to use two or more rime analogies, one based on the Clue Card from the story, and others based on Clue Cards from previous stories.

For example, the 'hay' rhyme family has lots of bisyllabic words in it. There are many words ending in both 'day' and in 'way'. Some of these words have onsets that can be worked out from the Alphabet Frieze, and rimes that can be worked out from familiar Clue Cards. Two examples are 'subway' (tub), and 'runway' (sun).

Always model the Clue Game for the children,

To make analogies between longer words

- Divide the word into syllables.
- Divide each syllable into onset and rime.
- Ask the children to work out the onsets using the Alphabet Frieze.
- Ask them to work out which Clue Cards they need for the rimes.
- Ask them to put the onsets and rimes together.

segmenting the target word into syllables, and then segmenting the syllables into onsets and rimes.

Links with other curriculum areas

'Shop' – hop

English/Maths Create a Grondle shop in the home bay. Goods can be made out of junk, salt dough, papier mâché, plasticine. Put prices on the goods, write notices about special offers, write/draw shopping lists and receipts. Count out money and give change. Who can buy the largest number of different things for 50p? How many different ways could you spend 10p?

PE/Maths **hop** Play hopping tag. How many hops can you do in one minute? How many hops to cross the classroom? Estimate, then count.

'Jam'

Maths Look at different jam containers (but be careful with the glass just in case of breakages). Which holds the most/least? How can we find out? Pour sand/water from one container into another, then pour sand/water into a third container and use this to compare how much each holds, or use a small cup to measure how many cupfuls each container holds.

Science Make some different flavoured jam tarts in cooking. Investigate your sense of taste and smell in an experiment. Can you guess the flavours when blindfolded? Record your findings. Which were the hardest/easiest to recognise? Compare your findings with a friend.

'Hay' – also 'day', 'tray' and 'play'

See also suggestions in Story Rhyme 4 where 'day' is a frequently used word.

English **play** Children can act out the story. They can record the lines onto a tape and then mime to the tape, or write their own script. They can create sound effects, large paintings for scenery and props. They can make posters, tickets, programmes, and invitations. They can perform the play to other children or to parents.

English Make a book sequencing the events from the story. This story has a happy ending, but discuss other possible endings (touch on the safety aspect of running away). Write or draw the other possible endings and include them all in the book by sticking the different versions as flaps at the back which the reader can then choose from.

English/Design Technology An alternative to the children acting themselves is to create a puppet play. They can use finger puppets, sock puppets, card characters stuck on the end of lolly sticks etc. Activities as above.

Maths **day** Days of the week as a sequence in time. If it is Monday today, how many days until Wednesday? If it is Sunday today, which day was it two days ago?

Put numbers of items on a tray. Play guessing games

– how many pencils are on the tray, etc.

Maths **tray** Develop estimation skills. Put numbers of items on a tray and play a guessing game, such as how many of one item are on the tray. Estimate then count and see whose guess was the closest.

Maths/History Children could make a survey of games played during playtime and find out the most popular games. They could then do a survey of the games played by their parents/grandparents and compare their findings. They could make up a new game and try to make up instructions for how to play the game (PE).

A talking point can be how to make the game fair and safe. Why should rough games be avoided in busy playgrounds? Who can play the game, just older children/my friends/boys? How do people feel if they are not included in a game, how did Little Troll feel? Can we change the game to include everyone, so that young children and children with disabilities can join in too? (Reference to disabled Olympics.)

'Troll'

Design Technology Make a finger-puppet troll. Cut out a small legless version of a troll and decorate. Attach a small rubber band to the back, just above where the legs should be. The child then sticks two fingers through the rubber band so that they are below the card cut out and can act as the troll's legs.

Alternatively, make a moving troll. Cut out a troll body minus arms and legs. Attach arms and legs with butterfly clips.

English Write letters to Little Troll (develop her as a pen pal as she is obviously looking for friends). The teacher can write replies back on behalf of Little Troll. Perhaps she could explain who the Grondles are and create a family tree. Children could add the new Grondle characters devised for the Rhyme activities (see above).

Geography/English What job do you want to do when you are older? Interview people in the school to find out what kind of work they do, e.g. cook, caretaker, head. What questions should be asked, how will we record the answers (use a tape recorder)? What sorts of things do the adult Grondles do? Which Grondle job would you prefer? Why? Children could take turns to mime one of the characters while the others guess which Grondle it is.

Maths Make things the right size for a baby troll and then one of the Grondle trolls, e.g. a chair from construction kits, a bed from junk. Compare their sizes.

Rhyme families in Story Rhyme 5

shop

top	copy	opposite
stop	topic	opera
drop	proper	popular
crop	copper	tropical
pop	popcorn	lollipop
cop	hopper	
chop	poppy	
mop	shopper	
prop	sloppy	
plop	topple	
flop	raindrop	
slop	treetop	
sop	workshop	
lop		

jam

am	hammer	family
Sam	camel	diagram
swam	bamboo	Miami
dam	mammoth	enamel
ham	ambush	kilogram
clam	camper	trampoline
ram	hamster	champion
slam	shampoo	
gram	mammal	
yam		
cram		
sham		
dram		
tram		
pram		

hay

may	maybe	yesterday
way	saying	Saturday
say	player	anyway
play	crayon	holiday
lay	daydream	runaway
stay	away	nowadays
pay	always	everyday
clay	today	underway
bay	Sunday	
May	okay	
ray	Norway	
gay	doorway	
pray	railway	
spray	delay	
jay	runway	
day	subway	
tray	dismay	
Ray	hallway	
stray	hurray	
nay		
Kay		
sway		
slay		
fray		
bray		

wig

big	signal	signature
dig	ignore	dignity
pig	wiggle	ignorant
fig	zigzag	indignant
twig	giggle	ignition
jig	digger	enigma
rig	wigwam	figurehead
brig	igloo	
sprig	pigtail	
gig	wriggle	
swig		

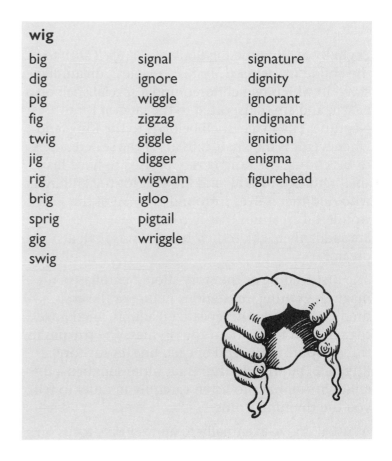

NB Some of the words in the lists may be unfamiliar to the children. However, they have been included so that you can use them later as a basis for extension work.

The Spell Shell focuses the children's attention on the **crab**, **swim**, **knot**, and **bell** rhyme families.

A list of rhyme family words is given on p. 55.

Introducing the Story Rhyme

Begin by reading the Big Book of *The Spell Shell* to the children. *The Spell Shell* is a magical, dream-like story, in which two children find a special shell on a beach, and are transported to the land of King Neptune. The magic shell belongs to the King, and whenever it is blown, it calls all of the sea creatures to his court. The King is very pleased to have his shell returned to him, and blows it for the children, who find themselves surrounded by all of the wonderful creatures that live in the sea. Then they are suddenly back on their beach – was it all a dream?

The first reading of the story should emphasise the magical, exciting, mysterious nature of the children's adventure. On repeated readings, encourage the children to listen for the rhymes. The rhymes in this story are at the end of each line, as in Story Rhyme 5, but the rhythm is far more subdued – the children will have to listen carefully in order to tell you the rhyming words.

As usual, move eventually to an exclusive focus on the sounds of the family words, using guided response questions (see Story Rhyme 1, p. 17).

The Spell Shell also makes extensive use of alliteration. There are lots of onsets that use S or that begin with S ('sk', 'sl', 'sw', 'sh'), to give a sense of the sea and of swishing water. This is another teaching point (see Onset section below).

Checking narrative comprehension

- Why did the girl think that she had found a special shell? Did it look special?
- What happened when she blew into the shell?
- How could the shell have called the sea-horses? Where did they come from? Are sea-horses real animals?
- Could the horses talk to the children? What did they say?
- Where did they take the children?

and so on.

You can also reinforce the story and the rhyme families by making links with other areas of the curriculum (see ideas at the end of this section).

Links to other ORT stories

You could read stories about the seaside or magic adventures. ORT stories you could use are: *On the sand*, *At the seaside*, *The cold day*, and any of the 'magic key' adventures, beginning with *1 The magic key*.

Developing phonological awareness

Use the reinforcement activities suggested in Story Rhyme 1 (p. 17) to consolidate awareness of the phonological patterns in *The Spell Shell*. Then develop this awareness with work on onsets, rhymes and analogies.

Onset work

Salient onsets in *The Spell Shell*

sl sk sw sp sh cr b kn

The use of alliteration in *The Spell Shell* will help to extend children's appreciation of how sound can be used in poetry to create atmosphere. Read each verse through again, asking the children to listen for words that begin with 's'. Point out that the 'sss' sounds are not all the same. For example, in the first verse there are three different two-consonant onsets that begin with 's', as well as S itself. These are 'sl', 'sk', and 'sw'. Ask the children to tell you how these onsets differ.

Reinforce this point with the Clue Cards. Begin with the Clue Card for 'swim'. You can also use the Sound Picture Card for 'swing'. Ask the children to think of some other words that sound the same at the beginning as 'swim' and 'swing', following the guidelines in Story Rhyme 4 (p. 39). Ask them which two letters they would need to begin writing these words. You can do the same for the double-consonant onset CR (crab).

The other Clue Card onsets are 'b' for 'bell', and 'kn' for 'knot'. The Sound Picture Cards for 'bun' and 'bat' can be used as well as 'bell' to teach the onset 'b' (see Story Rhyme 4, p. 39).

The double-consonant onset 'kn' is a single sound, and should be taught in a separate session. Explain that some sounds are written with two letters. Ask the children which other sound they have learned that is written with two letters ('sh', from Story Rhyme 5). Now explain that 'kn' is like 'sh', because it uses two letters to write one sound. Other examples on the Alphabet Frieze are 'ch', 'wh', and 'th'.

However, 'kn' it is a bit different, because it sounds the same as the sound made by the single letter N. This means that we cannot tell whether a word is written with N or KN just by its sound. All these words sound the same at the beginning. We have to *learn* the words that begin with KN. However, this is quite easy, as there aren't very many. Frequent ones include 'knife', 'know', 'knee', and 'knock'.

Reinforcing the onset work

This oral work can be supplemented by adapting the ideas listed in the Onset section (p. 94) to the onsets used in *The Spell Shell*. Similarly, any of the Card Games in Set 1 can be played, choosing games at an appropriate developmental level, and the children can use the Alphabet Frieze, the Tabletop Alphabets, and the Alphabet Photocopy Masters. For example, p. 42 in the Alphabet Photocopy Masters works on the double-consonant onsets CH, TH, WH, and SH, and p. 49 works on double consonants that begin with S. You can also:

- Read the class some poems that use alliteration to create a mood, and think about which onsets they use to do this. Various titles in the Oxford Reading Tree poetry list would contain suitable poems.

- Talk with the children about words that make you think of the sea, because they have a

swishing sound like the waves. How can we describe the sea on a stormy day? (Swirling, smashing, splashing.) How can we describe the sea on a calm day? (Shimmering, silvery, silent.) Discuss which words begin with 's' on its own, and which sounds you can hear after the 's' for the other words (for the onset 'sw', you can hear a 'w' after the 's', for the onset 'sm', you can hear a 'm' after the 's', and so on).

- Use 'She sells sea shells on the sea shore' as a stimulus for tongue twisters. Use different onsets to make more tongue twisters.

- The children can think up some 'cr' adjectives to describe crabs. They could have 'creeping' crabs, 'crawly' crabs, 'crusty' crabs, 'crying' crabs.

- The children can invent alliterative sentences about what Biff saw for B. Biff saw a bear on a bicycle. Biff saw a big baboon with a banana. Biff saw a ball on the beach etc.

Extension work

Extend the oral work to letters:

- The children can make a big wall frieze of the sea, with big, crashing waves. They can write some adjectives to describe the waves (smashing, splashing), and pin them to the frieze.

- The children can add a beach to the wall frieze, with lots of different crabs on it. They can label the types of crabs (crusty crabs, crying crabs).

- The children can make a book about the letter B. They can each draw a page for the book (Biff begins with B, bear begins with B).

- The children can display their tongue twisters by writing them on tongues stuck on to paintings of faces, or the face of an appropriate animal (e.g. a shark).

These activities (and others from the Onset section) can be extended to any onsets in *The Spell Shell*. The children can play some of the Card Games in Set 3, and trace the relevant Alphabet Photocopy Masters.

Rhyme work

The Spell Shell has a simple rhyming structure, so the children should have no difficulty in picking out the rhymes when you re-read the story. Ask them whether they can remember the extra rhymes that they thought of for each clue word ('swim', 'crab', 'knot', 'bell').

Reinforcing the rhyme work

You can build on this work by supplementing it with some of the ideas in the Rhyme section (p. 97). Any of the Card Games in Set 2 can be played, choosing games at an appropriate developmental level, and the rhyme activities in the Story Rhyme Photocopy Masters can also be used (those coded 'L' use oral recognition of rhyme).

The children can make up some simple poems for the Clue Card words. 'I had a swim with Jim and Tim.' 'I heard the bell and gave a yell.'

Read some other poems about magical events, such as Oxford Reading Tree *Wizard Poems*.

Use a selection of Rhyme Picture Cards from the families already introduced. Sit the children in a circle and spread the cards face up in the centre. Say a word to each child in turn and ask them to find a picture which rhymes with that word.

Use the Rhyme Picture Cards for 'knot'. Add a selection of card sets from rhyme families used in earlier stories (e.g. pin, dog, cat, sun, cap, hen, fan, zip). Three or four families will be sufficient. Ask the children to find all the cards that rhyme with a particular word (e.g. hot, win).

Extension work

Link the oral work to rime spellings:

Extend the Picture Card Game to include the Rhyme Word Cards. The children have to match the picture and the word.

The children could play Bingo. Use a selection of pairs of Rhyme Picture Cards and matching Rhyme Word Cards chosen from the families already introduced and some counters. Make the Bingo boards by placing the Rhyme Picture Card from each pair on blank grids (or use the bingo board in the photocopiable resources, see p. 117). The Rhyme Word Cards are placed in a box and players take turns to pick out a card. If players have the picture card on their board which matches the word on the card chosen, then they put a counter over that picture. The winner is the first to cover all the pictures on their board.

Use a selection of Rhyme Picture Cards and matching Rhyme Word Cards from the families already taught to create a simple board game (6–8 pairs should be enough). Design a board with a start and a finish (a board game for this activity is provided as a photocopiable resource, see p. 119) and spread the Word Cards face-up

around the board. The children throw a dice to move along the board, but before moving, they have to take a Rhyme Picture Card from the pile and say what it is. Then they have to find the matching word before they can take their go.

Alternatively, the Rhyme Picture Cards can be used for a more difficult game in which the children have to have a go at spelling the word on a chalkboard, wipe board, or in a sand tray before moving their counter. They can use the spelling pattern of the relevant Rhyme Word Card to copy if they get stuck.

Other activities at the end of the Rhyme section also involve spelling patterns, and these can also be adapted to the rhymes in *The Spell Shell*. The child-ren can also play some of the Card Games in Set 4, and complete the rhyme activities in the Story Rhyme Photocopy Masters for further consolidation and assessment (those coded 'Rw' focus on writing rimes).

Using analogies

Begin by playing the rhyming version of the Clue Game for the Clue Cards 'swim', 'crab', 'knot', and 'bell'. Play the game on different days for the different rhymes.

Reinforcing the analogy work

Supplement the Clue Game work for each rhyme family with other Analogy activities (see p. 99). Any of the Card Games in Sets 3 and 4 can also be played, and the pages in the Story Rhyme Photocopy Masters requiring the children to make analogies.

Help the children to create some 'rhyming lists'. Give each child one of the Clue Cards, and ask the children to write a list of rhyming words to match it. Encourage them to use the Alphabet Frieze to help them. The number of lists, and thus the number of rhyming families, can then be increased by swapping Clue Cards. Alternatively, the children could make the rhyming lists on a computer.

Adapt the Bingo game to analogies. Use a selection of rhyming (not matching) sets of three Rhyme Picture Cards and one Rhyme Word Card chosen from different families (knot, pin, dog, cat, sun, cap, hen, fan, zip) and some counters. Make the Bingo boards by placing the Rhyme Picture Card from each set on blank grids. The rhyming Rhyme Word Cards are placed in a box and players take turns to pick out a card. If players have a picture card on their board which rhymes with the word on the card chosen, then they put a counter over that picture. The winner is the first to cover all the pictures on their board. Make the game more difficult by restricting it to Rhyme Word Cards only.

Adapt the board game on page 119 to analogies. Use a selection of Rhyme Picture Cards and rhyming Rhyme Word Cards from the families already taught. This time the children have to take a Rhyme Picture Card from the pile and find the rhyming word before they can take their go.

Alternatively, the Rhyme Word Cards can be used for a more difficult game in which the children have to think of a rhyme for their card and then have a go at spelling the word on a chalkboard, wipe board, or in a sand tray before moving their counter. They should be encouraged to use the Clue Cards from the Word Tree to help them if they get stuck.

Extension work

Extend the analogy work to bisyllables for the clue word crab. Use words based on Clue Cards from earlier Story Rhymes. More able children can work out how to read these longer words by finding the correct pair of Clue Cards, and then using the Alphabet Frieze (see Story Rhyme 5, p. 47).

Long words with familiar rimes		
rabbit	crab +	hit
cabin	crab +	pin
tablet	crab +	net
habit	crab +	hit
inhabit	pin +	crab + hit

Links with other curriculum areas

'Knot' – also 'dot', 'pot', 'robot'

Art **dot** Painters often use dots of paint to make their pictures. Make a picture by printing with cylinders (e.g. corks) and thus making a dotty picture.

Art Tie dye. Cut an old white cotton sheet into squares. The child picks the square up from the centre and ties string around the cloth. Immerse one end of the material in one colour of dye (e.g. food colouring) and the other in a different colour. Leave to dry then cut off string and flatten out cloth.

Art **pot** Make pots. Use clay to make thumb pots or coil pots. Use papier mâché over half a balloon to make larger pots.

Art/Science **dot** Use a pin to prick holes in a piece of paper to draw a set of pictures or letters. Show them to a friend and then see if he/she can tell which one it is by touch only.

Design Technology **robot** Make a robot out of junk materials. Use a simple electrical circuit to make its eyes light up. Let the children take it in turns to operate the circuit so that the eyes light up when it hears two rhyming words. Write/draw what your robot can do.

English You will need tags or cards with a hole punched in them and lengths of string. The teacher writes onsets on one set of tags and matching rimes on another set. Children take turns to find and read two tags which make a word when put together and use the string to tie them together. Use the tags in a display at the end.

'Bell' – also 'shell'/general theme of the seaside

Art **shell** Observational drawing of a range of different shells.

Maths **shell** Sort a collection of shells, use them to weigh things, e.g. a crayon weighs 3 shells, a pencil weighs 5 shells.

Maths/Science **shell** Create a feely bag with shells in. Can you remove the shells in size order? Can you remove a shell the same as this one? Use information books to discover the names of the shells. Why do animals have shells?

Music Listen to bells in music, e.g. tubular bells. Make a collection of bells such as hand bells, cow bell. Get the children to shut their eyes while one child chooses a bell and plays it. The others then open their eyes and one child tries to play the same bell as the first child.

Hand out the bells and then read the story. Children can only ring the bell when they hear a word that rhymes with a word decided upon by the teacher.

The seaside

Art Create a seaside panorama in a shoe box. Use sand, shells, tissue paper, pebbles, and the like.

Art Use watery paint and investigate blue and green colour mixing to create pictures of under the sea and the different sea creatures.

Art/English Make a postcard showing things found at the seaside and write about what you could do there on the other side.

Art/English Add different coloured powder paint to sand and use this to create pictures by spreading glue onto paper and then sprinkling on the sand. Create sand letters by writing a letter in glue and then sprinkling with sand. Can a friend guess your letter by only using touch?

English Do some sand writing. The teacher writes a word at the top of the sand tray (or on a board or card for child to copy) and the child writes a family of rhyming words underneath using analogy. Mistakes are not important as the tray can be shaken and it all disappears! (See also the games in Rhyme section above.)

Maths Data collection, recording, and interpretation. Children do a survey to find out who has been on holiday to the seaside. Display the findings on Venn diagrams, mappings, and graphs, and get children to describe the results. Get the children to bring in any postcards they have of the places they have visited and find the places on a map.

Music Use sand and junk materials to make shakers. Compose music to represent the sounds of the sea using your instruments. Start with a calm/stormy sea and change.

Science Compare wet and dry sand when making sandcastles. Which is better?

'Crab'

Design Technology Make a crab with moving claws. Draw the claws on card and cut them out so that they have a long strip of card at one end. Join the strips of card together like a pair of scissors with a butterfly clip. Cut out a crab body and attach over the handle part of the scissors, fixing to one handle only. Use the other free handle to make the claws move.

P. E. Crabs move along close to the ground and are very good at moving sideways. Can you move like a crab? How many different ways can you find to move about close to the ground (such as rolling, crawling, slithering)? Crabs have ten legs – eight touching the ground and two as pincers. How many parts of your body are touching the ground in each case? Find ways to balance with different numbers of parts of your body touching the ground. Work with a friend to find different ways you can balance together with eight parts touching the ground between you.

Maths **grab** How many bricks, conkers, shells, dominoes etc can you grab and hold in one hand. Estimate first then count. How many will you be able to grab if you use two hands? Do a survey to find out who in the class has the biggest 'grab'.

'Swim'

Science Investigate whether different materials sink or swim (try and get some polystyrene packing balls as one of the materials, as these are similar to children's floats). Can we decide in advance which materials will swim? How? Why do we use floats at the swimming pool to keep our heads above water? What might they be made of?

Maths/Geography Data collection, recording, and interpretation. Record the information about which materials floated using an appropriate method. The children can do a survey to find out who can swim, and record the results.

Geography Where do people go swimming? Why is it safer to swim in a swimming pool than in other bodies of water? Discuss ways to keep safe in and around water. Look through magazines and make a collection of pictures of different bodies of water such as rivers, lakes, seas, canals.

Rhyme families in Story Rhyme 6

swim

him	simple	important
Jim	himself	similar
Tim	limit	limited
rim	timber	imitate
slim	timid	criminal
dim	mimic	impatient
trim	shimmer	chimpanzee
skim	victim	timidly
grim	denim	
Kim	pilgrim	
brim		
prim		
whim		

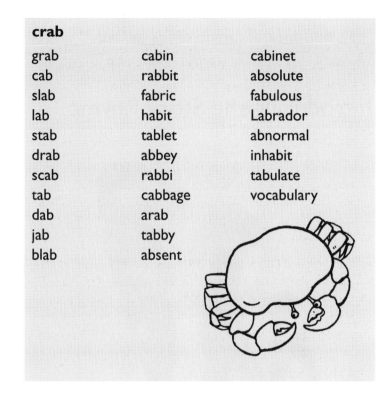

crab

grab	cabin	cabinet
cab	rabbit	absolute
slab	fabric	fabulous
lab	habit	Labrador
stab	tablet	abnormal
drab	abbey	inhabit
scab	rabbi	tabulate
tab	cabbage	vocabulary
dab	arab	
jab	tabby	
blab	absent	

knot

not	bottom	forgotten
got	cotton	lottery
hot	bottle	apricot
lot	otter	hypnotic
spot	potter	hippopotamus
shot	cannot	
dot	forgot	
pot	robot	
plot	teapot	
slot	mascot	
trot	parrot	
cot	pilot	
jot	carrot	
blot	ballot	
rot	maggot	
clot		
tot		

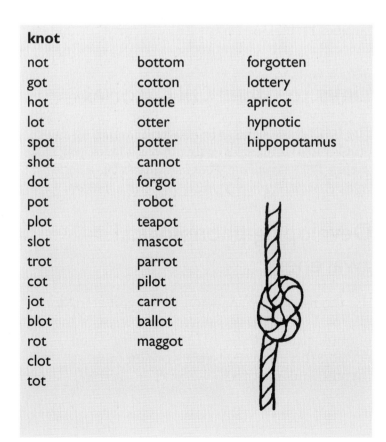

bell

tell	shellfish
spell	telltale
fell	doorbell
sell	farewell
cell	yellow
smell	cellar
shell	jelly
hell	hello
yell	cello
swell	bellow
dwell	
knell	
Nell	
quell	

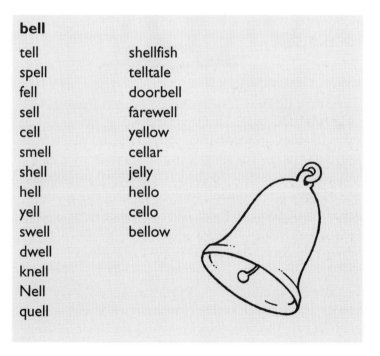

NB Some of the words in the lists may be unfamiliar to the children. However, they have been included so that you can use them later as a basis for extension work.

That's *nothing!* focuses the children's attention on the **bag**, **hill**, **duck**, and **mum** rhyme families.

A list of rhyme family words is given on p. 61.

Introducing the Story Rhyme

The Story Rhyme *That's nothing!* has an irregular rhyming structure. The rhyming words occur at the ends of lines, but not always in the same place from verse to verse. This means that the children will have to concentrate to find all the rhyming words when they are listening to you reading the story. It also means that, as the reader, you will have to read each verse with a slightly different rhythm, since each is deliberately idiosyncratic! Try and place most emphasis on the rhyme words as you read.

Begin with the Big Book. Read the story slowly to the children, so that they can imagine the events in each verse. *That's nothing!* is based on two children who are boasting to each other about the amazing things that their mothers can so. As one child boasts, the other builds up a mental picture of a mother carrying out these superhuman actions. In the children's imaginations, the mothers enact cumulatively more fantastic and improbable feats, and teen at the end of the story the mothers are revealed to be quite ordinary – capable of losing keys and having bicycle punctures!

The imaginary events that the mums perform are always depicted in thought bubbles. Point these out to the children as you read, and discuss this narrative convention. On repeated readings, point to key elements in the pictures as you stress the rhymes. For example, in the first verse you would point out 'crag', 'flag', and 'bag'. Move on to an exclusive focus on the sounds of the family words, using guided response questions (see Story Rhyme 1, p. 17).

Checking narrative comprehension

- What is a mountain crag? Why do people put flags on them?
- Could you really parachute with a paper bag? Why not?
- Could you really ski with a tray of soup? What's a 'loop-the-loop'? Do we usually 'loop-the-loop' on skis?
- Would it be easy/hard to lift a ten-tonne truck? What else is very heavy?
- Why do wrestlers use special throws?

and so on.

You can also reinforce the story and the rhyme families by making links with other areas of the curriculum (see ideas at the end of this section).

Links to other ORT stories

The following ORT stories, covering amazing mums (and grans!) and apparently amazing feats, might be useful: *Biff's aeroplane, Poor old Mum!, The weather vane, 4 Gran, A monster mistake, Good old Mum.*

Developing phonological awareness

Use the reinforcement activities suggested in Story Rhyme 1 (p. 17) to consolidate awareness of the phonological patterns in *That's nothing!* Then develop this awareness with work on onsets, rhymes, and analogies.

Onset work

> **Salient onsets linked to _That's nothing!_**
>
> **b d h m**

The irregular and idiosyncratic rhyme pattern used in _That's nothing!_ does not highlight any particular onsets. However, as in Story Rhyme 4, you can still use the story as a starting point for onset work by using the Clue Cards. The onsets of the clue rhymes used in _That's nothing!_ have all been encountered before, and so this repetition provides valuable consolidation and reinforcement of the onsets learned in Story Rhymes 2, 3, 4, and 6.

Use the Clue Cards in the ways suggested in Story Rhyme 4 (p. 39), using the story and the pictures as a source of other words with shared onsets. Also use the Alphabet Frieze, and ask the children to tell you which other Clue Cards have the same beginning sounds as 'bag', 'hill', and 'duck'.

> **Clue Cards which share these onsets**
>
> **duck** dog dad day
> **bag** bed bell
> **hill** hen hit

Prior work with the onset 'm' was based on Mrs Moore (Story Rhyme 2) and mouse (Story Rhyme 2, and on the Alphabet Frieze). The children may well remember this, if not, you can remind them.

Reinforcing the onset work

You can now supplement this work in a number of ways. As usual, the Alphabet Frieze, Alphabet Photocopy Masters, Tabletop Alphabets, and Card Games (Set 1) all provide support activities. There are also lots of ideas in the Onset section.

The children can think of lots of adjectives to describe mums on different occasions. For example, they could have a 'magic' mum (when the mum has created a special treat), a 'muddled' mum (when the mum has forgotten something), a 'mad' mum (when the child is naughty), a 'miserable' mum (when the child is ill), and so on.

The children can think of a variety of foods that begin with the onsets on the Clue Cards. They could choose bread, butter, baked beans, broccoli, bananas, melon, mangoes, mandarins, mustard, ham, honey, and so on. The children have to make up an imaginary lunch box, but they can only include foods that begin with 'b', 'd', 'h', and 'm'.

Play a class game of 'I Spy', but restrict it to the sounds 'b', 'd', 'h', and 'm'. The children take it in turns to spy something in the classroom that begins with one of these sounds. Stress that they are _only_ allowed to select items with these sounds. The others have to guess what they are thinking of, and check adherence to the rules.

Extension work

Extend this oral work to letters:

The children can make a class book describing 'My mum'. They can illustrate the alliterative sentences invented in the oral work (mad mum, etc.), and write the onset words beneath each picture.

NB. As some children will be cared for by adults other than their mums, you could introduce activities based around story-book mums.

The children can create a food frieze for the letters B, D, H, and M. They can draw pictures of the foods that were in their lunchboxes, write the names of the foods underneath each item, and group them around each letter on the frieze – perhaps in four big lunchboxes.

Use the Sound Picture cards for 'b', 'd', 'h', and 'm'. Ask the children to sit in a circle, and put the cards face-up in the middle of the group. Trace a letter on the back of each child in turn. The child has to choose a picture which begins with the sound that was traced on their back.

Use the Sound Picture Cards and the Letter Cards for the onsets 'b', 'd', 'h', and 'm', and a Snakes and Ladders board (one is provided as a photo-copiable resource, see p. 120 – 1). Shuffle the cards into a pile, and put the pile face-down in the centre of the group. Play as for Snakes and Ladders. When the children land on a ladder, they have to pick a card. If it is a Sound Picture Card, they have to give the correct letter for the sound before going up the ladder. If it is a Letter Card, they have to think of a word beginning with the sound of the letter before going up the ladder.

As usual, any of the other activites in the Onset section (p. 94) can be adapted to these onsets, and the Alphabet Photocopy Masters provide further scope for consolidation and assessment. The children can also play some of the Card Games in Set 3.

Rhyme work

Re-read the Story Rhyme, asking the children whether they can remember the Rhyme Family rhymes in each verse. You can prompt them by asking them to supply the rhyming word in the critical lines of the story, or by reading out one verse at a time and asking the children to spot the rhymes. You can then use the Story Rhyme as a basis for further rhyming work by asking the children to invent simple poems about their own mums or other adults important to them. These can be as short as two lines.

> My mum is very tall
> She makes me feel extra-small!
>
> My mum has long dark hair
> But dad's and mine is blonde and fair.

If they have difficulty in thinking of something to make a rhyme about, give them a topic. What does their mum do after they go to school? Does their mum go to work? What does she like to cook? If necessary, you can supply a first line for them to complete.

> My mum goes to the shops every day
> She says she never has time to play!
>
> My mum goes to work by bus
> If she's late there's quite a fuss!
>
> My mum likes to cook me eggs
> She says they'll give me long, strong legs!

The poems needn't make much sense — the important activity for the children is to think about rhyming words. You could also adapt the 'silly poem' theme discussed in Story Rhyme 4 (p. 40) with the children, by changing the activities of the fictional mums in amusing ways.

> I don't want to brag
> But if there's a snag
> My mum can solve it
> With a paper bag!
>
> How's this for a thrill?
> My mum got a drill
> And drilled right through
> My window sill!

Reinforcing the rhyme work

You can build on this work by supplementing it with some of the ideas in the Rhyme section (p. 97). Any of the Card Games in Set 2 can be played, and the rhyme activities in the Story Rhyme

Photocopy Masters can also be used (those coded 'L' are based on oral recognition of rhyme).

Another way to reinforce the oral rhyming work is to continue the 'mum's rhymes' theme, either by using the children's rhymes about their own mums, or by using the silly rhymes based on the fictional mums.

- The children can paint a picture of themselves with a thought bubble depicting their rhyme about their mum. For example, the child who feels extremely small beside their very tall mum could paint themselves as 'normal' size, with a thought bubble containing their very tall mum with a very short self standing next to her.

- Different children can memorise different verses of the Story Rhyme. Other children then mime the actions as they speak. For example, children can mime skiing downhill with a tray of soup! They can mime the 'silly poem' rhymes as well, for example drilling through a window sill.

- Use the Rhyme Picture Cards as a basis for creating more poems, this time based on the Clue Card 'hill' (pill, mill, drill). The children have to invent a poem that uses two of these pictures. It doesn't matter if the poems are extremely simple ('I stood on the hill, to see the mill') – the act of producing a poem will still have a beneficial effect. This poetry game can be extended to other Rhyme Picture Cards as well.

Extension work

This involves linking the oral work to the rime spellings:

- The children can write their two-line poem about their mum in their best writing. The poems can either be attached to the paintings, or can be inserted into the thought bubbles. The pictures can then be used to form a wall display.

- Use the Rhyme Word Cards for 'hill'. Ask the children to select the correct word cards for the rhyme that they invented using the Rhyme Picture Cards. For example, the child who invented 'I stood on the hill to see the mill' should select the Rhyme Word Cards 'hill' and 'mill'. This activity can be made more difficult by including some wrong cards, which still share some of the correct sounds (for example, 'hall' and 'men'). It can also be extended to the Rhyme Word Cards for any other Rhyme Picture Card poems that were created.

Other activities at the end of the Rhyme section also involve spelling patterns, and these can also be adapted to the rhymes in *That's nothing!*. The children can play some of the Card Games in Set 4, and use the Story Rhyme Photocopy Masters for further consolidation and assessment (those coded 'RW' involve writing rimes).

Using analogies

Play the rhyming version of the Clue Game for the Clue Cards 'duck','hill', 'mum', and 'bag', playing the game on different days or in separate sessions for each of the Rhyme Families.

Reinforcing the analogy work

Supplement the Clue Game with other Analogy activities from the Analogy section (p. 99), adapting them to the rime families in *That's nothing!* The Story Rhyme Photocopy Masters provide further opportunities for consolidation and assessment, and the children can play the Card Games in Sets 3 and 4.

Ask the children to make some rhyming lists for the different Clue Cards. You can either ask them to write words that use onsets from the Alphabet Frieze, or add some double-consonant onsets that should be familiar from previous Story Rhyme work. These include: 'bag' (snag, scrag); 'mum' (swum, scrum); 'hill' (swill, skill, grill, trill); 'duck' (truck, cluck).

The children will need to use the Alphabet Frieze and the rime patterns from the Clue Cards to spell the words. For the double-consonant onsets, they will need to find the correct onsets by referring to their earlier work (for example, by going back to the Mungle Flap story for 'sn', 'tr', 'cl', 'gr', and 'scr'.

Photocopy some of the verses from the Story Rhyme, and stick white paper over the Rhyme Family words. Ask the children to fill in the missing words without copying from the book. They can use the Clue Cards to help them. This will require them to match onsets from the Alphabet Frieze to the appropriate rimes.

Extension work

Extend the analogy work to bisyllables for the different clue words (see Story Rhyme 5, p. 47).

Long words with familiar rimes	
magnet	bag + net
ragged, jagged	bag + bed
maggot	bag + knot
zigzag	wig + bag
fillet, skillet, millet	hill + net
trumpet, crumpet	mum + net
minimum	pin + i(igloo) + mum
bucket	duck + net
unlucky	sun + duck + y
Kentucky	men + duck + y

Links with other curriculum areas

'Mum' – 'drum'

Art Make a mobile of mums with their parachutes.

English Ask the children to make an individual book about their mum (e.g. My mum is great because . . .). Sensitivity to the potential variation in the make-up of different children's families is essential. The children could also be encouraged to make books about different family members.You could also use some of the mums' activities in the Story Rhyme as a basis for extension work, for instance parachutes, as above.

Music Make rhythms on drums, or on home-made drums, e.g. up-turned plant tubs. Try to drum the rhythms of nursery rhymes or Story Rhymes already covered, such as *The Mungle Flap*.

Science Test different materials to see which makes the best parachute. Which material falls fastest/slowest? Make a fair scientific test by cutting pieces of material to the same size. Use the results of the test to design and make a parachute for a mum in the story.

'Hill'

Geography Make a collection of postcards showing different geographical features, e.g. lakes, mountains, hills, deserts, cities. Ask the children to sort the cards and explain their decisions. What is the same/different about these cards? Where would you like to live, where would you like to go on holiday, where would you like to go shopping? Why? What is the same/different about where you live and the place in the cards? How would you get to school/your friend's house/the shops if you lived there?

Science Why does most skiing take place in hilly places? Look at pictures in skiing brochures if you can get some. Investigate the effect of slopes by making your own hills. Place some boxes under one end of a board or thick card. Make a steeper hill by placing more boxes under another board. What happens when you place a toy truck on the ground where there is no slope? What about the first hill, or the second hill? Mark how far the truck moves each time with a counter. Make another hill and predict how far you think the truck will go. Record your findings.

'Bag' – 'flags'

Art **flag** Use a piece of white cotton and a stick to make a flag. Decorate the cotton using fabric crayons, felt-tip pens, tie dye, or dip 'n' dye techniques.

Design Technology Make a collection of paper and plastic bags. Which bag is the strongest? Which bag would be best in the rain? Design a fair test to answer these questions.

Design Technology/Art Create a logo to advertise a class shop. Make recycled paper bags from scrap paper, e.g. folded and stapled along the sides. Print the design on the paper bags by e.g. press printing – transfer the design to a piece of polystyrene using a blunt pencil, consider what you need to do to print the design the correct way round. Use a roller to apply paint to the polystyrene and press down onto the bag.

'Duck' – 'truck'

Extensions based on birds – see 'hen' activities under *The Mungle Flap* Story Rhyme. For 'truck' see transport activities in *Supersonic engine juice*. Link also to bikes.

Art Observational drawing of a bike.

Maths Data collection, recording, and interpretation. Get the children to do a survey to find out who has a bike or other item. Display the findings on Venn diagrams and mappings, and get children to describe the results.

Science Why are feathers used in quilts and duvets? What other materials do we use to keep us warm? Test several different materials to see which are good at keeping things warm. Get several plastic bottles which are all the same and fill them with hot water. Wrap each bottle in a different material such as cotton, nylon, wool. Leave one bottle unwrapped. Leave for about half an hour then see which bottle has kept the water the warmest.

Rhyme families in Story Rhyme 7

hill

will	village
still	silly
Bill	filling
fill	pillow
till	hilly
kill	miller
skill	chilly
bill	villa
mill	shilling
ill	fillet
drill	pillar
shrill	skilful
Jill	illness
chill	hillside
sill	downhill
thrill	windmill
spill	fulfill
pill	standstill
grill	billboard
dill	million
twill	
frill	
trill	

bag

flag	wagon	magnetic
drag	magnet	magazine
tag	dragon	agony
rag	ragged	dragonfly
nag	jagged	stalagmite
brag	dagger	octagonal
crag	jaguar	magnificent
lag	maggot	
sag	zigzag	
stag	handbag	
wag		
hag		
gag		
snag		

mum

sum	number	museum
drum	summer	minimum
gum	trumpet	maximum
hum	clumsy	
plum	jumper	
strum	tumble	
rum	umpire	
slum	bumpy	
bum	dummy	
chum	crumpet	
scum	grumpy	
swum	jumbo	
glum	crumble	
thrum	jumble	

duck

truck	lucky	luckily
struck	bucket	unlucky
luck	duckling	Kentucky
stuck	sucker	
buck	plucky	
chuck	pucker	
pluck		
suck		
tuck		
puck		
cluck		
muck		
shuck		

NB Some of the words in the lists may be unfamiliar to the children. However, they have been included so that you can use them later as a basis for extension work.

Rockpool rap focuses the children's attention on the **ball**, **snow**, **star**, and **knob** rhyme families.

A list of rhyme family words is given on p. 67.

Introducing the Story Rhyme

Rockpool rap has been written in a rap-style format. The regular and catchy rhythm should be brought out as you read, especially when you are reading the chorus. Try to use your tone of voice to create a rap mood. You could also accompany your reading by tapping with a pencil, clicking some castanets, or snapping your fingers to the rhythm – 'rapping' as you read! The rhythmic pattern is

> di, di, **da**
> di, di, **da**
> di, di, **da** di **da da da!**

The story centres on a clever clam called Clive, who keeps the other shellfish in his rockpool amused by his singing, jiving and twisting to his own guitar playing. Clive decides to adopt the name Elvis, and to seek his fortune beyond the rockpool in the open sea. The open sea turns out to be a rather unfriendly place, and his show is attended by hostile sharks and swordfish. Elvis decides to go home again, back to his sheltered and small rockpool where his barnacle fans are waiting.

On repeated readings, encourage the children to join in with the rap refrains, especially by supplying the rhyming words at the end of each line. The children could also try to provide the clicking and snapping to the rap rhythm during the chorus, although this may take some practice. Point out the different types of fish in the pictures, and some of the key concepts in the verses (such as the rockpool concert hall). Move on to an exclusive focus on the sounds of the rhyme-family words, using guided response questions (see Story Rhyme 1, p. 17).

Checking narrative comprehension

- What is a rockpool? How is a rockpool created by the sea?
- What kinds of sea creatures are there in the story?
- What kind of dancing might you be doing if you were jiving?
- Why do you think Clive changed his name? What name would you choose? Why?

and so on

You can also reinforce the story and the rhyme families by making links with other areas of the curriculum (see ideas at the end of this section).

Links to other ORT stories

If you like, bring in other stories about people who have left home and either made their fortunes, or failed to make their fortunes (e.g. *Dick Whittington*). ORT stories about 'showing off' include: *Kipper the clown* and *The weather vane*. Performances of varying success feature in *Bull's eye! Poor old Mum!*, and *The headache*. Stories connected to a seaside theme include: *The cold day* and *At the seaside*.

Developing phonological awareness

Use the reinforcement activities suggested in Story Rhyme 1 (p. 17) to consolidate awareness of the phonological patterns in *Rockpool rap*. Then develop this awareness with work on onsets, rhymes, and analogies.

Onset work

> **Salient onsets linked to Rockpool rap**
> **s st sh sn sw cl kn**

Although the rhythm of *Rockpool rap* does emphasise some onsets (for example, 'cl', 'sh', 's', 'st'), we will focus on those that are on the Clue Cards, particularly 'sn', 'st', and 'kn'. You can also use 'sw' (swim in Story Rhyme 6) as *Rockpool rap* enables you to draw the children's attention to the set of double consonants that begin with S (the onset 'cl' features in Story Rhyme 9).

Begin with the Clue Cards for 'snow' and 'star', using the reinforcement activities suggested in Story Rhyme 4 (pp. 39), and adding the Clue Card 'swim' from Story Rhyme 6. When you use the story as a source for shared beginning sounds, you could say that the children's job is to listen out for words beginning with a 's' sound. You could divide the children into three teams, each with a special mission to listen out for the 'sn' words, the 'st' words, or the 'sw' words. Alternatively, you could ask all of the children to raise their hands each time that they hear a 's' word, and then to tell you which Clue Card has the same initial sound.

Some of the words that they find will be new S-onsets ('sl','sm', 'scr'). When you ask the children which letters they would need to write the sounds 'sn', 'st', and 'sw', elongate your pronunciation to emphasise that there are two letters in each onset (s-n, s-t, s-w). Do the same for any new 's' onsets that they discover.

The other teaching point to reinforce concerns the onset 'kn', in which two letters represent a single sound (*phoneme*). This onset was first learned in Story Rhyme 6 ('knot'). Repeat the teaching sequence from Story Rhyme 6 (p. 51), using both 'knob' and 'knot' to illustrate your points, as well as the Alphabet Frieze.

Again, you can bring in 'sh' as another example of two letters that are used for one sound. Stress that 'sh' is different from the other S-onsets that you have been learning – SH represents a single sound.

Reinforcing the onset work

You can now supplement this work in a number of ways, using the Alphabet Frieze, the Alphabet Photocopy Masters, the Tabletop Alphabets, and Card Games (Set 1). There are also lots of ideas in the Onset section (p. 94), which you can adapt to the onsets in *Rockpool rap*.

- Play a class game of 'I Spy', adapting it to things in the classroom that begin with double/treble-consonant onsets starting with S (STory book, SNakes and ladders, SCRapbook , etc.). Alternatively, adapt the 'I Spy' game so that the children have to *describe* objects whose names begin with a double-consonant onset starting with S (I'm thinking of something long and thin

that slithers along the ground which you can see in a zoo – SNake).

- The children can take it in turns to think of other characters or objects that live in Elvis's rockpool. The characters or objects have to have alliterative names (Billy Barnacle, Linda Limpet, Roland Rock, Sunil Seaweed, etc.).

- The children can think up some names for the Shellfish Jive, or for Elvis's backing group. Needless to say, the names should use alliteration (The Funky Fish Reel, The Crazy Crabs, etc.).

Extension work

Extend the oral work to letters:

- The children can cut out some large letters S from sugar paper. Then they can search through a selection of old magazines to find pictures of things that begin with S. They can cut them out, and stick them onto their letter. Ask them to draw a ring around any picture that has a double-consonant onset, and to write the correct pair of letters beneath it.

- Attach one of the double-consonant onsets beginning with S (ST, SN, SP) onto the door of the classroom or homebay. The children have to say a word beginning with the chosen onset as they leave or enter the classroom.

- Play the Clue Game for Onsets for the onsets 'st', 'sn', 'sw', 'sl', and 'sm' (see Story Rhyme 3, p. 32):

Onsets with familiar rimes

ST	stub stun stay stop stab stag stuck
SN	snip snub snap snot
SW	swam sway swig swop swell swot swill swum (*exceptions*: swan, swab)
SL	slip slog sled slit slam slay slop slab slim slot slum slob slow
SM	smog smell small
Clue Cards	zip fan tub dog bed cap lid hit sun wig jam shop hay swim crab knot bell bag hill mum duck ball snow

The Clue Game onset work can also be extended by using some of the other activities in the Onset section. There is also a page in the Alphabet Photocopy Masters that practises S-onsets (p. 49).

Rhyme work

The most obvious basis for further rhyming work in *Rockpool rap* is rap itself! Read through the Story Rhyme again, emphasising the clicking, snapping rhythm, and asking the children for the key rhymes. They could also do the clicking and the snapping for you. Now supplement this rhyming work by asking the children whether they know any raps. Ask them to invent some raps of their own. Useful themes for the children's raps include 'Schoolhouse Rap', or 'Playtime Rap'. Base the raps on the hip-hop rhythm used in *Rockpool rap*:

> Rockpool rap!
> Rockpool clap!
> Do the starfish hip, hop, hap!

You could provide the chorus to help the children to get going:

> Schoolhouse rock!
> Schoolhouse roll!
> Do the swinging classroom stroll!
>
> Playtime here!
> Playtime now!
> Hear that bell go, wow wow wow!

It doesn't really matter if the raps that the children create are utter nonsense – as usual, it is the experience of manipulating the sounds, rhymes, and rhythms of spoken language that is important.

Reinforcing the rhyme work

You can build on this work by supplementing it with some of the ideas in the Rhyme section (p. 97). Any of the Card Games in Set 2 can be played, choosing games at an appropriate developmental level. Two of the Clue Cards in this Story Rhyme have associated Rhyme Picture Cards and Rhyme Word Cards, 'star' and 'ball'. The rhyme activities in the Story Rhyme Photocopy Masters can also be used (those coded 'L' are based on oral recognition of rhyme).

Another obvious way to reinforce the rhyming is to continue the rap theme using mime and other dramatic devices. This will further consolidate the rhythm and rhyme of the children's raps.

- The children can record their different raps on tape.
- The children can mime to the raps that they have created. Other children can provide appropriate percussion for the 'hip-hop' rhythms. The raps can either be recited live or mimed to the tapes.

- The children can put on a rap show for each other. Groups of children can present their raps to the rest of the class. Each group will need a chief rapper to conduct the dialogue, someone to provide the rhythm by clicking and snapping, and a set of willing actors!
- Alternatively, the whole class can present *Rockpool rap* to the rest of the school. Different children can memorise one verse each, and take it in turns to be the chief rapper. The whole class can join in for the choruses. One child can be Elvis, and the rest can act out the different roles from the rockpool and the wide open sea.

You can also use the Card Games in Set 2 and some of the other activities in the Rhyme section or in the Story Rhyme Photocopy Masters for further work.

Extension work

As before, this involves linking the oral work to rime spellings:

- The children can make a rap songbook for the whole class. They can each write out a verse of 'The Schoolhouse Rap' or other raps that have been invented, using their best writing. These can then be collected into a rap songbook for the whole class to enjoy.
- If the class presents *Rockpool rap* to the rest of the school, they could make song-sheets for the choruses, so that all the other children can join in with the rap. The children can each copy out a different chorus, and these can be photocopied and distributed to the audience.

Other activities at the end of the Rhyme section also involve spelling patterns, and these can also be adapted to the rhymes in *Rockpool rap*. The children can play some of the Card Games in Set 4, and use the Story Rhyme Photocopy Masters for further consolidation and assessment (those coded 'RW' involve writing rimes).

Using analogies

Play the rhyming version of the Clue Game for the Clue Cards 'ball', 'snow', 'star' and 'knob', playing the game on different days for each family.

The rime family for 'snow' has some important exceptions. The rime 'ow' can either be pronounced to rhyme with 'snow' or with 'now' (cow, how, allow, etc.). This point should be explicitly mentioned during the Clue Game (see the Rhyme family list, p. 67, for other exceptions).

There is also a single exception for the 'ball' family, which is 'shall'. However, the pronunciation in 'shall' is also used in some bisyllabic words (see the Rhyme Family list, p. 67).

Reinforcing the analogy work

Supplement the Clue Game with other Analogy activities from the Analogy section, adapting them to the rime families in *Rockpool rap*. The Card Games provide further opportunities for consolidation, and there are some analogy activities in the Story Rhyme Photocopy Masters.

Photocopy or copy out different verses of *Rockpool rap*, leaving gaps for the rhyme family words. The children have to write the correct words in the gaps, using the Clue Cards and the Alphabet Frieze to help them.

Make a 'word ball' for the 'ball' family (see 'word wheel' instructions on p. 116). Useful onsets for the ball include C, F, H, T, W, SM, and ST. Ask the children to copy out the words that they can make with the ball, and to use each one in a simple sentence.

Extension work

Extend the Clue Game to bisyllables (see Story Rhyme 5, p. 47).

Long words with familiar rimes	
beggar	leg + star
popular	shop + u + star
vinegar	pin + leg + star
hallway	ball + day
snowball	snow + ball
fallen	ball + men
window	pin + snow
pillow	hill + snow
robin	knob + pin
goblin	knob + pin

Another useful clue word is 'her'	

This is a good point at which to introduce the clue word 'her'. 'Her' is the only monosyllabic word with the rhyme 'er' in English, but it has the largest rime family of any English word, with 1,908 members. As this word is not picturable, its spelling pattern needs to be memorised.

caller, taller	ball + her
rower, mower	snow + her
robber, cobbler	knob + her

Links with other curriculum areas

'Star'

Design Technology Stick foil stars on a black background. Create day and night in the classroom by drawing the curtains and shining a torch onto your stars.

Maths Make stars out of card, write rhymes on the stars, and make them into a mobile. Five pointed stars can be made by drawing round a pentagon and extending the sides. Six pointed stars can be made by drawing round two overlapping equilateral triangles.

Other cultures Find out about Tanabata, the Japanese star festival.

Science Discuss the sky at night. What can you see in the sky? How far away do you think stars are? (You could also discuss astrology, and the important role that certain cultures place on its predictions.)

'Ball'

An associated theme for work in other curriculum areas is provided by the seaside, shells, and fish – see *The Spell Shell* for some ideas.

Maths Play number bingo, drawing numbered balls or counters from a bag.

Design Technology Make a skittle. Scrunch a large piece of newspaper into a ball for a head, leaving one end for a neck. Push the neck into the top of a plastic bottle and tape the head, to the bottle. Cover the bottle with papier mache and leave to dry. Paint the skittle and stick on hair and material for clothes. Try knocking your skittle over with different types of ball, such as foam, wool, plasticine. Which is the most effective ball? Record your findings.

Science/PE How many different ways can you move a ball/get the ball to your partner, e.g. roll, throw, kick, bounce. How can you make the ball move faster/slower/stop? Experiment with some simple ball activities, e.g. throwing a ball into a bin, rolling a ball between your friends' legs, kicking a ball into a goal.

'Snow'

Art Make snowflakes by folding circles in half and half again, then cutting out small segments. Unfold and look at the symmetrical pattern.

Geography Where in the world does it snow? Where is it always snowing? Where doesn't it ever snow? Why not? Why is there snow on Christmas cards? What do Christmas cards in hot countries show (most show snow scenes!)? Collect some pictures of snow scenes (e.g. from Christmas cards, postcards, skiing holidays, and ski brochures). Attach them onto a world map.

Maths Use a pegboard/squared paper/geoboard/plastic shapes to make a symmetrical pattern. Make part of a symmetrical pattern for a friend to finish.

Science What happens to water when it gets very cold? What happens to snow/ice when it gets hot? Make some ice cubes. Find the best place to keep the ice cubes from melting – place the cubes in different locations and check on them throughout the day. What happens if you put coloured ice cubes in a large jar of warm water?

Science Look at symmetrical patterns in nature. Symmetrical patterns the children might be able to think of in nature are flowers, leaves, shells, butterflies.

Rhyme families in Story Rhyme 8

knob

job	problem	probably
Bob	object	obvious
rob	robin	obstacle
mob	hobby	obsolete
sob	robber	obligate
bob	lobster	obtain
blob	wobbly	
cob	cobbler	
snob	goblin	
throb	cobweb	
lob	oblong	
fob	gobble	
slob	wobble	
hob		

star

far	sugar	similar
car	dollar	familiar
bar	solar	popular
jar	polar	nuclear
tar	collar	circular
scar	cellar	vinegar
mar	beggar	particular
spar	vicar	peninsular
tsar	nectar	
par	altar	
char	burglar	

snow

know	slowly
show	lower
grow	snowy
low	mower
blow	snowflake
slow	below
flow	follow
throw	window
row	yellow
bow	farrow
glow	fellow
crow	shadow
tow	arrow
mow	hollow
sow	pillow
stow	rainbow
[how	swallow
now	elbow
cow	scarecrow
row	aglow
bow	
brow	
wow	
prow	
sow	
vow]	

ball

all	ballroom
small	hallway
call	football
tall	rainfall
fall	recall
wall	nightfall
hall	snowball
stall	eyeball
gall	overall
squall	calling
mall	falling
pall	fallen
thrall	tallest
[shall]	caller
	[balloon
	Sally
	valley
	ballet
	rally
	fallow]

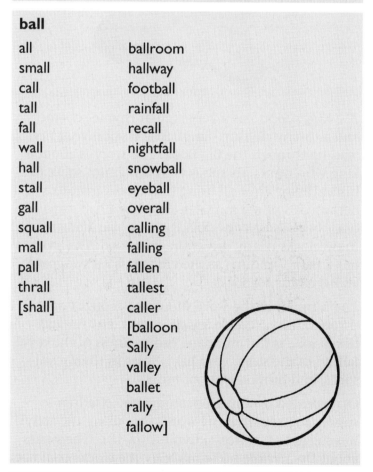

NB Some of the words in the lists may be unfamiliar to the children. However, they have been included so that you can use them later as a basis for extension work.

The King's socks focuses the children's attention on the **clock, king, plug,** and **flash** rhyme families.

A list of rhyme family words is given on p. 74.

This is the first Story Rhyme where we segment the onset and the rime into phonemes.

Introducing the Story Rhyme

The King's socks has a very regular rhyme scheme and a catchy rhythm. Emphasise this on your first reading through the Big Book. The story is about a king who wants his subjects to bring him socks for his birthday. They all bring him clocks instead, because his prime minister, who has a bad head cold, hears 'socks' as 'clocks'. The noise made by all these clocks nearly drives the king mad. The story has a happy ending, as the king ends up swapping all his clocks for socks.

The humour of the story should be brought out through tone of voice, exaggeration, etc. An additional joke is the mundane ordinariness of the royal family in the story, who have holes in their royal socks, and drink tea out of mugs.

On repeated readings, encourage the children to supply the key rhyming words etc., using the activities suggested in Story Rhyme 1 (p. 17). The verses about the terrible noise made by the clocks could be memorised by the whole class.

 Said the King, 'I can't sleep
 For the bong and the bing
 And the tick and the tock
 And the chime and the ping' etc.

Checking narrative comprehension

■ Why did the King think that everyone would want to give him presents on his birthday? Do we give Queen Elizabeth presents on her birthday?

■ Why did the Queen suggest asking for socks?

■ What was the matter with the King's prime minister? Why can it be difficult to hear when you have a cold?

■ What did the Prime Minister tell everyone to buy?

and so on.

You can also reinforce the story and the rhyme families by making links with other areas of the curriculum (see ideas at the end of this section).

Links to other ORT stories

The style of this Story Rhyme is reminiscent of the nonsense verse of Lewis Carroll (e.g. 'The Hunting of the Snark') and of Edward Lear. Other nonsense poems of this kind could also be read to the class, with accompanying discussion of how to make words and nonsense words fit the rhyme pattern of a story or a poem.

ORT stories with odd characters include: *Castle adventure, Underground adventure, It's not fair* and *The laughing princess.* Stories about new clothes could be used: *New trainers, Yasmin's dress,* or *Fancy dress.*

Developing phonological awareness

Use the reinforcement activities suggested in Story Rhyme 1 (p. 17) to consolidate awareness of the phonological patterns in *The King's socks.* Then develop this awareness with work on onsets, rhymes, and analogies.

Onset work

Salient onsets linked to *The King's socks*
c p fl k

Although the regular rhyme pattern used in *The King's socks* does not emphasise any particular onsets, the Clue Cards for Story Rhymes 8–12 have been chosen to enable direct teaching of frequently encountered double-consonant onsets. The double-consonant onsets featured in this Story Rhyme all use L as a second consonant: 'cl', 'fl' and 'pl'. Some of these should already be familiar from Story Rhyme 3, as the rhyming structure used in *The Mungle Flap* drew attention to the onsets 'fl', and 'cl'. Repetition of these onset patterns here will help to consolidate learning.

Teach these onsets by using the Clue Cards (see Story Rhyme 4, p. 39). As in Story Rhyme 8, ask the children to tell you the beginning sounds of the words slowly, in an elongated fashion, so that you can hear the two sounds separately. Ask them which letters they would need to write the beginning sounds of these words.

Extension: Oral onset segmentation

You can extend this work by segmenting the onset into its constituent phonemes.

- Say the clue words together ('clock', 'flash', 'plug'), emphasising the two initial sounds ('c – l', 'p – l', 'f – l').
- Ask the children if they can hear a sound that is always the same at the beginning of these different words. What is it?
- Ask the children whether they can think of any other words where the second sound at the beginning is 'l'.
- Nominate some yourself, asking the children which sound they can hear in front of the 'l' (e.g. 'bl' – blue, black, blast; 'gl' – gloomy, glen, glowing; 'sl' – slippery, slow, slide).

Reinforcing the onset work

This oral work can then be supplemented in a number of ways. There are a few pages in the Alphabet Photocopy Masters that practise these onsets (pp. 44, 47, and 48). As usual, the Alphabet Frieze, Tabletop Alphabets, and Card Games (Set 1)

can all be used as a basis for support activities. There are also lots of ideas in the Onset section.

- The children can make up sentences using words beginning with'cl', 'pl', or'fl' (*Floppy saw a fly on a flower*).
- Alternatively, they can use two of the onsets in the same sentence (*Please don't pluck the flowers*), or even all three (*Clever Clara plucks some flowers. Floppy is playing with a clock.*'
- The children can play 'add a word' for one of the onsets ('I went shopping and I bought some flour, a flag, a fly swatter, a bunch of flowers', etc.).
- Alternatively, you can make the game more difficult by asking the children to use each onset in turn, 'fl', 'pl', 'cl', ('I went shopping and I bought some flour, a plug, a clock, a flag, a plastic gnome, a toy clown', etc.).

Extension Activities

Link sounds to letters by playing the Clue Game for Onsets (see Story Rhyme 3, p. 32).

Onsets with familiar rimes
CL clan clip club clog clap clam clop clot cluck clash
PL plan play plop plot plum pluck
FL flan flip flat fled flog flap flit flop flab flag flow fling flock
Clue Cards zip fan tub cat dog bed cap hit jam shop hay crab knot bag mum duck snow flash king clock

Encourage the children to use the Clue Cards to work out the words that you use for reading analogies, or that they nominate for spelling analogies.

Segmenting onset spellings

Finally, have a teaching session in which you emphasise the shared L in all three onsets, and link it to spelling. You could use the following procedure:

■ Put the three Clue Cards at the top of the board. Write their words in plastic letters, leaving a gap between onset and rime.

■ Ask the children to tell you which sound they can hear in front of the 'l' sound in each word as you place them on the board.

■ Segment the onset further into its separate consonants, showing them how each constituent sound links to the letters. Use open-ended questions. ('That's right, the sound in front of the 'l' in 'plug' is 'p'. Which letter do we use to write that sound? That's right, we use P. P makes a 'p' sound, and L makes a . . . ? Yes, a 'l' sound. So P – L spells . . . ? That's right, 'p'-'l'.')

■ Now create three lists of words for the three onsets, placing a word in each list in turn (reading analogies). In each case, segment the onset, and discuss its spelling, using open-ended questions. Alternatively, ask the children to nominate words for the list (spelling analogies).

■ Ask the children to read/spell each word for you, using onset and rime analogies.

If you use a reading-analogies approach, you can begin by using shared rime words (e.g. 'an' in clan, flan, plan). This will highlight the sounds of the shared onsets. You can put the relevant Clue Cards for each rime at the side of the board (e.g. fan).

CL, FL, and PL words with the same rimes

clan	flan	plan
clop	flop	plop
clip	flip	
cluck		pluck
clog	flog	
clap	flap	
clash	flash	
cling	fling	
clay		play
clot		plot

Clue Cards zip fan cap shop hay dog
knot duck flash king

As the children get the hang of the game, you could ask them how you would write other –L words that rhyme with each set (e.g. clot, plot – slot, blot, etc.).

Careful attention to the individual sounds (phonemes) in the onsets and the rimes of words is crucial for the further development of good reading and spelling skills.

The Clue Game onset work can also be extended by using some of the other activities in the Onset section (p. 94).

Rhyme work

Read *The King's socks* to the children again, emphasising the rhyming patterns and the rhyming words. Ask them to supply the rhymes at key points in each verse, and to recite the 'clock noise' verses themselves.

Reinforcing the rhyme work

As usual, any of the other ideas in the Rhyme section (p. 97) can be adapted to the rhymes used in *The King's socks*. Similarly, any of the Card Games in Set 2 can be played, choosing games at an appropriate developmental level. The rhyme activities in the Story Rhyme Photocopy Masters can also be used (those coded 'L' are based on oral recognition of rhyme).

The children can play rhyming Kim's Game, using the Rhyme Picture Cards for the 'clock', 'plug', and 'king' families. Place these twelve cards (or a subset of them) on a tray. Ask the children to study them, and then remove one. The children have to tell you which one is missing.

Use the Rhyme Picture Cards for the 'clock', 'plug', 'king', 'knot', and 'hill' families. Introduce a hand puppet whose name rhymes with one of the rhyme families (the puppet can be made out of a sock – see section below on Links with other curriculum areas). The children take it in turns to pick out the cards that the puppet likes because they rhyme with his or her name.

Use a selection of Rhyme Picture Cards which includes the 'clock', 'plug', and 'king' families. Sit the children in a circle, and place the cards face-down in the centre. The children take it in turns to pick one of the cards, say what it is, and think of something that rhymes with it.

Extension work

Extend the oral work to rime spellings.

- The children can play rhyming Kim's Game, the puppet game, or the 'sitting in a circle' game with the Rhyme Word Cards instead of the Rhyme Picture Cards. It may be necessary to cut down on the number of cards if the children find any of these games too difficult.

- The children can play Bingo, the caller using the Rhyme Picture Cards for the 'clock', 'plug', and 'king' families, and the players write rhyming words on the boards (see list of rhymes at the end of this section). A Bingo board is provided as a photocopiable resource (see p. 117). Use some extra Rhyme Picture Cards from other families if you want a bigger board. The caller selects the pictures one by one and calls them out, and the children place counters on the rhyming words on their boards.

Other activities at the end of the Rhyme section also involve spelling patterns, and these can also be adapted to the rhymes in *The King's socks*. The children can play some of the Card Games in Set 4, and use the Story Rhyme Photocopy Masters for further consolidation and assessment (those coded 'RW' involve writing rimes).

Using analogies

Play the rhyming version of the Clue Game using the Clue Cards for 'clock', 'king', 'flash', and 'plug'. Play the game on separate days for the different families.

Reinforcing the analogy work

Supplement the Clue Game with other Analogy activities from the Analogy section (p. 99), adapting them to the rime families in *The King's socks*. Some of the activities in the Story Rhyme Photocopy Masters also involve analogies.

- Use a selection of Rhyme Word Cards drawn from the 'fan', 'zip', 'cap', and 'knot' families, and the three double-consonant Clue Cards from the Story Rhyme (clock, flash, plug). Spread the cards face-down in front of the children. The children take it in turns to pick a card and to read the word on it. Then they have to think of a word which rhymes with the word on the card,

which must begin with either CL, FL, or PL, and try to spell it on a wipe board. They should be encouraged to use the spelling pattern of the relevant Clue Card as well as the rime on the card that they have chosen to help them.

> You can also focus on the clue word 'king' as the rime 'ing' is a very useful one. As well as being the rime in many monosyllabic words (ring, thing, sing), it also forms the present participle (shopp*ing*, sing*ing*, danc*ing*).

Draw the children's attention to the dual role of 'ing' by asking them to think of words that use the 'ing' rime as a verb ending ('action words'). Then ask them how to spell some of these 'ing' words. This can be done in the following ways:

- Ask the children to make up some verb lists ('action lists') for 'ing'. Give each child one or more of the Clue Cards, and ask them to write down all of the rhyming verbs that they can think of for each Rhyme family. For example, if a child is given 'fan' and 'zip', they could write 'banning', 'fanning', 'manning', 'tanning', 'scanning',' planning', and 'dipping', 'nipping', 'ripping', 'sipping', 'tipping', 'tripping'. NB. You will need to provide a lot of support for the children as some of the words are quite difficult and probably unfamiliar.

> An important teaching point to make is that we double the letter at the end of the first rime when we add 'ing'. So to make 'fanning' out of 'fan', we need to double the N; to make 'wetting' out of 'wet', we need to double the T; to make 'zipping' out of 'zip', we need to double the P; and so on.
>
> The only exceptions to this 'rule' are CK (picking), W (snowing) and Y (playing), and rimes that end in 'e' (making).

- If the children find the Clue Card lists too difficult, encourage them to write out the alphabet on a sheet of lined paper, omitting the vowels. Then they can think of an action word for each letter. They can write down any of these words that they can spell.

- Alternatively, direct them to verbs that they worked on in the Clue Game for Onsets with PL, FL, and CL (e.g. planning, flopping, clopping, clucking, plucking). This will further consolidate the onset work as well as teaching the 'ing' rime.

✎ Some verbs use the 'ing' rime in their rime stem. Help the children to think about these verbs, too, and ask them to work out how to spell them (e.g. singing, flinging, clinging, ringing, slinging).

Segmenting rime spellings

The three Clue Card spellings 'clock', 'flash', and 'king' are more complex in structure than most of the clue words that we have learned so far. For these spellings, two letters are used to write a single final sound (the CK in 'clock', the NG in 'king' and the -SH in 'flash'). Two letters representing one sound are known as digraphs. This fact can be explicitly demonstrated as a teaching point. This is the beginning of work that segments the rime.

Begin by working with 'flash' and 'clock' (the consonant digraph NG features in Story Rhymes 10, 11, and 12 as well). You could use the following procedure for each clue word:

- Put the Clue Card at the top of the board. Spell the word in plastic letters, segmenting the onset and the rime.
- Ask the children for the sounds of the vowel and the consonant digraph, using open-ended questions. (Each consonant digraph has a *single* sound.)
- Segment the rime into its vowel and final consonants, keeping the consonant digraph together. Ask the children to tell you how each sound links to the letters.
- Ask them to think of other words that have the sound of the consonant digraph in them (spelling analogies). It doesn't matter whether they think of word-initial or final examples (e.g. SH – shop, clash). Alternatively, make other words using SH or CK, and ask the children to work out what you are writing (reading analogies).
- Ask them to read/spell each word for you, using onset and rime analogies.

In each case, always explain that some words use two letters to write one sound. When you are talking about 'clock', you can remind them of the Clue Card word 'duck', which also uses the two letters CK at the end. Stress that CK is never used at the *beginning* of words. Ask them which letters *are* used to make the 'k' sound at the beginning of words (C and K). Point the letters out on the Alphabet Frieze.

Later Story Rhymes use the rimes 'ack' and 'ick', 'ong', 'ang', and 'ung', and 'ush', so you will have the opportunity to emphasise all of these teaching points again. Keep the initial sessions in which you work on segmenting the rime fairly short.

Links with other curriculum areas

'Clock' – 'sock'

Design Technology Use junk or construction kits to make a clock with moving hands, e.g. a grandfather clock could be made out of decorated boxes with the hands attached with a butterfly clip. Recite the nursery rhyme 'Hickory Dickory Dock' and make a card mouse run up and down your clock, using a piece of string.

English Sequence the events of the story using language associated with time, e.g. first, next, then.

Geography Where are there clocks in school/your home/in the town? Why are they there? Where else would be a good place for a clock? What do the clocks look like? Is there a clock like that in the story?

Maths What do clocks measure? What can you do in one/three/five minutes? Carry out an investigation, e.g. use egg timers to measure time and find out how many letters you can write/how many bricks you can make into a tower/how many beads you can thread/how many hops you can do in the time. In a longer time will you do more or fewer? Estimate first, then count and find out.

Maths/Design Technology Use cubes or sticks to make the numerals you see on digital clocks. Alternatively, make a timer. Use the lid from a large coffee jar. Stand it on its side and push it. What happens? (it rolls). Now place a piece of plasticine to one side of the lid and push it. Now it rocks instead of rolls. What can you do before the rocker stops moving? An egg timer can also be made by making a small hole in the lids of two drink bottles that are the same size. Sellotape the bottles together. What can you do before the sand runs through the hole? What happens if the hole is made bigger/smaller?

Maths Discuss what happens during the day and how we know when to get up/go out to play/go to lunch/go home. What are the most important times in the day? Illustrate the important times of the day and add clock faces showing the time. Sequence the pictures in the correct order and turn them into a frieze or book. Children can make their own little books showing what they do in the morning, afternoon, and evening.

Music/PE Play an instrument like the tick-tock of a clock. Ask the children to move on their feet in time to the instrument. The clock can speed up, slow down, or stop as it is wound up and runs down. Can the children listen and move in time to the instrument?

'Sock'

Art/Design Technology Make a sock puppet who is a character from the story. The puppet can like words that rhyme and the children can make their puppet say rhyming words or sort and collect rhyming pictures or objects (see play activities in *Who wants to play with a troll?*).

Maths Counting in twos. How many people are wearing socks today, how many socks are there? Make a display using pairs of socks to illustrate counting in twos: e.g. 1 person wearing socks has 2 socks; 2 people wearing socks have 4 socks; 3 people wearing socks have 6 socks. Get the children to interpret the display by asking questions such as 'if there are 3 people wearing socks, how many socks are there altogether?' and 'if there are 4 socks, how many people can wear a pair of socks?'

Science Matching-by-touch game. Make a collection of pairs of socks. Put one of each sock in a pile and muddle them up. Take turns to pick one of the matching socks, shut your eyes and try to find its partner in the pile by touch only. What does the sock you are searching for feel like? Encourage the child to describe what the socks feel like, e.g. is it soft, is it fluffy, is it rough or smooth?

'Plug' – 'mug'

Art Make a mug out of clay. Shape the clay over a paper-covered jar, use a coiling technique, or simply gouge out a mug shape from a solid lump. Which mugs look better? Which are easier to use?

Maths Make a collection of mugs and sort/count them.

'King'

History/English/Geography Does the King live in an old or a new building? How can you tell? What differences can you find between your house and the King's castle? (The historical theme can be extended to touch on English history if this Story Rhyme coincides with a class visit to a local castle, or some other local interest/occasion can be linked in). Do we have a king or a queen? Who is our queen? Who will be the next king? What is a prince? Which princes do we have? Are princes always young boys? Why not? What about some other countries? Does America have a king?

History Compare stories about real and fictional kings and queens. Show photographs of present royal family and compare with photographs/portraits of past kings and queens. How are their clothes different? Why aren't there any photographs of Queen Elizabeth I?

See day activities in *Bad day, good day* for birthday.

'Flash' – dash

English **dash** Play a dash word game like 'hangman'. Write a list of words you want the children to practise on a large sheet of paper. Include several each of 2, 3, 4, and 5 letter words. Each child takes a turn to pick a word without letting anyone else know what it is. They then draw a dash to represent each letter on a wipe board or chalk board. The other children take it in turns to say a letter they think might be in the word – using your sheet of words to help them. If the letter does occur in the word, the first child writes it in on the correct dash. If the letter does not occur, the child can draw one line of an outline of a king's castle (instead of the traditional hangman). The child wins if the castle is completed before the other children have made up the whole word. An extension of the activity is to play without the help of your sheet of words.

Rhyme families in Story Rhyme 9

clock

rock	pocket
block	rocky
stock	rocket
lock	cockpit
shock	jockey
dock	locket
knock	socket
flock	hockey
cock	peacock
mock	unlock
sock	
chock	
tock	
crock	
hock	
frock	

plug

dug	ugly
rug	rugged
drug	buggy
jug	juggle
bug	smuggle
tug	luggage
snug	nugget
hug	snuggle
mug	humbug
shrug	
lug	
chug	
slug	
smug	
pug	
thug	

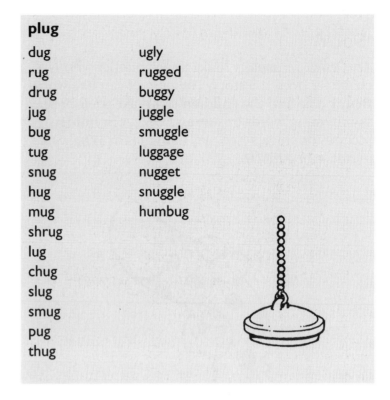

flash

cash	fashion
crash	cashier
splash	flashlight
dash	cashmere
ash	bashful
slash	eyelash
sash	flashy
hash	haberdasher
smash	
trash	
mash	
lash	
clash	
rash	
gnash	
gash	
brash	
thrash	
bash	
stash	

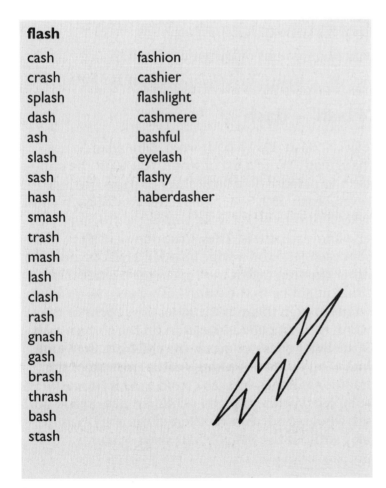

king

thing	kingdom
sing	singer
bring	singsong
spring	something
ring	morning
string	evening
swing	clothing
wing	lightning
cling	
sting	
fling	
sling	
wring	
ding	

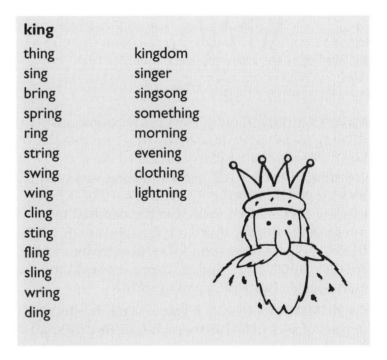

NB Some of the words in the lists may be unfamiliar to the children. However, they have been included so that you can use them later as a basis for extension work.

Gran, Gran! focuses the children's attention on the **sack**, **long**, **brush**, and **dress** rhyme families.

A list of rhyme family words is given on p. 79.

Introducing the Story Rhyme

Gran, Gran! has a very regular rhyming scheme and rhythm, which is easy to bring out by putting stress on appropriate words. The story is about an apparently scatty Gran, who appears to spend a lot of time at the shops buying a large number of rather eccentric items. These things bear no relation to the items actually requested or needed by her family. At the end of the poem we realise that Gran has known what she was doing all along – she was buying all the things for herself!

Begin with the Big Book. Many of the important rhymes are shown or repeated in the illustrations, so point these out as you read. Bring out the humour of the story in your tone of voice – the increasingly impossible items that Gran keeps buying require the use of exaggerated intonation. The denouement should also be emphasised – it reflects on the rather self-centred family, and comes as a big surprise to them.

On repeated readings, ask the children to supply the key rhymes as you point to the items in the pictures etc., using guided response questions (see Story Rhyme 1, p. 17).

Checking narrative comprehension

■ What did Gran buy when she went to town?

■ Why is the little boy/mummy/daddy upset?

■ Can you take things back to shops? Will they give you your money back?

and so on.

You can also reinforce the story and the rhyme families by making links with other areas of the curriculum (see ideas at the end of this section).

Links to other ORT stories

Gran is a favourite character in ORT stories. You could read *4 Gran*, *A monster mistake* and *The great race*. Shopping features in *The pet shop*, and *Adam goes shopping*. Characters get in a muddle in *The lost teddy* and *The foggy day*.

Developing phonological awareness

Use the reinforcement activities suggested in Story Rhyme 1 (p. 17) to consolidate awareness of the phonological patterns in *Gran, Gran!* Then develop this awareness with work on onsets, rhymes, and analogies.

Onset work

Salient onsets linked to *Gran, Gran!*

gr   br   dr

The regular rhyming scheme used in *Gran, Gran!* does not highlight any particular onsets. Once again, however, onset work can focus on the Clue Cards. The double-consonant blends 'br', 'gr', and 'dr', used on the Clue Cards for 'brush' and 'dress', and in *Gran's* name, provide a useful opportunity for thinking about double-consonant onsets ('gr' is also on the Alphabet Frieze for Gran).

Onsets that use R as a second letter are quite frequent in English (the others are 'cr', 'fr', 'pr', and 'tr'). The onset 'cr' is used in one of the Clue Cards for Story Rhyme 11 (cross), and 'gr' recurs in Story Rhyme 12 (grass), enabling further reinforcement.

As usual, start with the Clue Cards (see Story Rhyme 4, p. 39). Some work on 'gr' was done in Story Rhyme 5 (Grondles), and the children may remember this, too.

Extension: oral onset segmentation

Follow the procedure suggested in Story Rhyme 9 (p. 69). Use the Clue Cards for 'dress' and 'brush', and add 'Gran' as well. Bring in other –R onsets (crab, pram, troll, fry), and ask the children which sound they can hear in front of the 'r' sound in each word.

Reinforcing the onset work

This oral work can then be supplemented in a number of ways. There are a few pages in the Alphabet Photocopy Masters that practise the –R onsets (pp. 43, 45, 46). As usual, the Alphabet Frieze, Tabletop Alphabets, and Card Games (Set 1) can all be used as a basis for support activities. The ideas in the Onset section (p. 94) can also be adapted to the onsets used in *Gran, Gran!*

- The children can play an 'add a word' game about what Gran bought when she went shopping. Gran can only buy things that begin with 'gr' ('Gran went shopping and she bought green eggs, a great big coat, a greasy bag of chips, etc'.).
- The children can make up some alliterative sentences for 'br'. ('I had some brilliant brown bread.' 'Bring your brown brushes to Brands Hatch, etc.')
- The children can make up some sentences about what they took to the dry cleaners for 'dr'. ('I went to the dry cleaners, and I took some droopy drawers.' 'I went to the dry cleaners, and I took a dark-blue dress, etc.)'

Extension activities

Link sounds to letters by playing the Clue Game for Onsets (see Story Rhyme 3, p. 32).

Onsets with familiar rimes	
BR	bran brat brim brag brash bring
DR	drip drop drab drag drill drum drug
GR	gran grip grub grin grog grid grit
	grab grim grill grow
Clue Cards	**zip fan tub cat pin dog lid**
	hit shop crab swim knot
	bag hill mum snow plug
	flash king

The children should now be able to work out both the onsets and the rimes of many words for themselves.

Segmenting onset spellings

Finally, have a teaching session in which you emphasise the shared 'r' in all three onsets, and link it to spelling. Use the procedure outlined in Story Rhyme 9, p. 69.

The Clue Game onset work can also be extended by using some of the other activities in the Onset section (p. 94).

Rhyme work

Take up the Big Book to read with the children again. The regular rhyme pattern used in *Gran, Gran!* should help the children to remember the story. If they do, you could read the story with them by providing the first two lines in each verse yourself, and then allowing the children to finish the verse off for you. You could point to the pictures of the relevant items to help them.

Given the simple verse structure of *Gran, Gran!*, a useful supplementary rhyming activity is to change each verse in amusing ways. You can preserve as much or as little of the original as you choose:

> Gran, Gran, you made a mistake,
> When you went shopping in town.
> This vegetable rack
> Is all red and black,
> The one that I wanted was brown!
>
> Gran, Gran, come quick as you can,
> You've got in a bit of a mess!
> I didn't want custard,
> I wanted some mustard,
> To make an egg sandwich with cress!

Reinforcing the rhyme work

You can build on this work by supplementing it with some of the ideas in the Rhyme section (p. 97). Any of the Card Games in Set 2 can be played, choosing games at an appropriate developmental level. The rhyme activities in the Story Rhyme Photocopy Masters can also be used (those coded 'L' are based on oral recognition of rhyme).

Another obvious way to reinforce this work is to extend the theme of Gran's rhyming shopping, either by using the Rhyme Picture Cards, or in other ways:

- Give the children a selection of the Rhyme Picture Cards to use in a shopping rhyme about Gran. You could use the 'ring', 'mug', 'clock', 'ball', 'jar', and 'pill' cards. Their job is to pick a card, and then to use it in the shopping rhyme.

For example, if they choose the clock, the rhyme could be:

Gran, Gran, come quick as you can,
You've got in a bit of a mess!
I didn't want *clocks*,
I asked you for *socks*!
And whose is this mustard and cress?

The children can play a game about Gran going shopping for rhyming items. They can use a selection of Rhyme Picture Cards, none of which rhyme with each other. You can place the cards face-up at the end of a hall, and then you, or another child, can be Gran. Gran calls out words that rhyme with the different pictures, saying 'I went shopping and bought a . . . '. Pairs of children take it in turns to race and find the card which rhymes with the word called by Gran.

Extension work

Extend the oral work to rime spellings:

Play the running game based on *Gran* using the Rhyme Word Cards instead of the Rhyme Picture Cards.

The class can make their own Story Rhyme about Gran. Each child can write out and illustrate one of the rhymes that they invented during the oral activities. These can be bound together into a class book.

Other activities at the end of the Rhyme section also involve spelling patterns, and these can also be adapted to the rhymes in *Gran, Gran!* The children can play some of the Card Games in Set 4, and use the Story Rhyme Photocopy Masters for further consolidation and assessment.

Using analogies

Play the rhyming version of the Clue Game using the Clue Cards 'sack', 'long', 'brush', and 'dress'. Play the game on separate days for the different families.

Reinforcing the analogy work

Supplement the Clue Game with other Analogy activities from the Analogy section (p. 99), adapting them to the rime families in *Gran, Gran!* The Card Games provide further opportunities for consolidation, and there are some Analogy activities in the Story Rhyme Masters.

The children can make up some rhyming shopping lists for Gran. The Rhyme Picture Cards can be used as before. However, this time the children will need to *write* both the name of the picture on the card (e.g. clock) and the name of something that rhymes with it (e.g. sock).

Photocopy or copy out different verses of *Gran, Gran!*, leaving gaps for the rhyme family words. The children have to write the correct words in the gaps, using the Clue Cards and the Alphabet Frieze to help them.

Make a 'flip book' for the 'sack' family (see p. 115). Use the onsets BL, CR, TR, ST, SN, SL, and SH. The children have to copy out the rhyme words, and then decide which onset letter they can leave out to create another rhyme to write underneath. For example, for 'black' they could make 'back', for 'track' they could make 'rack', and so on.

A more difficult version of this game can be played by asking the children to find another Clue Card that they can use to match the onset of the flip-book words to create a new word. For example, for *black* they could use *clock*, giving *block*, for *track* they could use *flash*, giving *trash*, and so on. They should be encouraged to use the spelling pattern of the relevant Clue Card as well as the onsets in the flip book to help them.

Extension work

Extend the Clue Game to bisyllables (see Story Rhyme 5, p. 47).

Long words with familiar rimes	
fatness	cat + dress
witness	hit + dress
unless	sun + dress
madness	sad + dress
jacket	sack + net
cracker	sack + her
haystack	day + sack
unpack	sun + sack
oblong	knob + long
longer	long + her
longing	long + king

Segmenting rime spellings

The Clue Card spellings in Story Rhyme 10 again demonstrate complex rime spellings in which two letters make a single final sound. These are the '-sh' in 'brush', the '-ng' in 'long' and the '-ck' in 'sack'. These complex spellings can be taught using the procedure in Story Rhyme 9 (p. 70). Bring in previous Clue Cards using the same consonant digraphs for reinforcement in each case (i.e. 'duck' and 'clock' for -CK, 'king' for -NG, and 'flash' for -SH).

Links with other curriculum areas

'Long'

Maths Find objects longer/shorter than e.g. a crayon. Sort objects and put them in order according to length. Alternatively, put objects such as pencils of different lengths in a feely bag. Can you remove the objects in order of length?

'Dress'

Art Make a collage of a fashion show. All the models can have dresses of different shapes and materials, or be dressed in different colours, styles (include boys!). Alternatively, make paper figures that you can dress in different clothes. The clothing can be drawn onto paper, coloured in, and then cut out, leaving extra 'tags' to attach to the paper figures. The figures can either require extensive wardrobes of dresses (e.g. model dolls), or can require particular kinds of functional clothing (e.g. policewomen, male nurses, etc.).

Science Investigate the best material for a dress (see ideas for **tub** in *Supersonic engine juice*).

'Brush'

Art Compare the kind of paint effects that can be created with the different brushes. For example, a stiff washing-up brush can be used to create different effects from a 'mop' type washing-up brush, a spongy make-up brush will give a different effect to a fine hair make-up brush, and so on.

Maths How many individual bristles are there in different types of brushes? Sort them into groups by estimating e.g. less than twenty/more than twenty. Discuss ways of improving estimates. Although the design of some kinds of brushes makes it impossible to count the bristles, for others we can make an approximate guess by an informed estimate. Use different brushes to explain estimation (e.g. in a hairbrush or stiff washing-up brush, we can count

the number of bristles in one nodule, and then multiply up by the number of nodules. Check whether two or three nodules have the same number of bristles. How close are they? As the number of bristles in a single nodule will probably vary, our estimate is only approximate).

If you wish, you can give examples of other estimating procedures (as in school fête games like guess the number of sweets in the jar). You can also extend the estimating theme to estimates of large numbers from samples. For example, how many cornflakes in a packet? We can estimate this by counting how many fit into a small cup, and working out how many cups there are in a packet.

Science What different kinds of brushes do we use in everyday life? Make a collection for the classroom (paintbrushes, hairbrushes, toothbrushes, washing-up brushes, dog brushes, make-up brushes, wire brushes, toilet brushes, etc.). What kinds of materials are used for the brush itself? For the handles?

'Gran'

Art Observational drawing of family members.

History Ask the children what makes a grandparent. Then ask them to describe their own grandparents – do they fit the stereotypes? Encourage the children to bring in photographs of their family members, and create a pictorial family tree. Discuss how the photographs differ. Create a family tree for the characters in the story.

Make a class time-line showing the years in which the children and their family members were born to show that older people have lived for more years.

Look at pictures of the children when they were born. How have they changed? What can they do now that they couldn't do then?, etc. Make little books showing what they could do as a baby, a toddler, and a five-year-old. Get the children to bring in objects from their babyhood and make a museum with labels, e.g. 'Charlotte played with this when she was two'.

English What could the Gran in the story want all the things that she bought for?

History/English Ask the children what they think schools would have been like when their grandparents went to school. How could they find out? Use information books, write letters to grandparents and interview grandparents, to find out.

Rhyme families in Story Rhyme 10

sack

back	package
black	jacket
Jack	backward
track	blackboard
pack	backbone
crack	cracker
lack	jackdaw
rack	attack
stack	horseback
shack	racetrack
jack	haystack
tack	unpack
snack	rucksack
quack	feedback
smack	hunchback
whack	
slack	
hack	
knack	
clack	
wrack	

dress

less	express	business
guess	unless	happiness
press	darkness	loneliness
stress	success	lioness
bless	princess	merciless
mess	address	bottomless
Bess	goodness	baroness
chess	illness	
cress	endless	
tress	helpless	
	sickness	
	witness	
	mattress	
	duchess	
	impress	
	confess	
	madness	

long

song	longer
strong	stronger
wrong	longest
gong	longing
throng	along
tongs	belong
thong	oblong
prong	headstrong
pong	

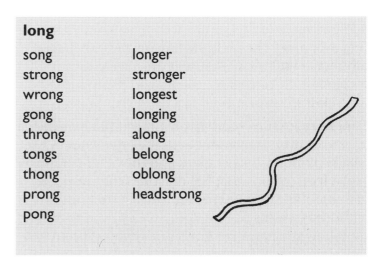

brush

rush	mushroom
hush	toothbrush
crush	[pusher
mush	cushion
lush	bushy
blush	rosebush
flush	ambush]
gush	
plush	
slush	
thrush	
[bush	
push]	

NB Some of the words in the lists may be unfamiliar to the children. However, they have been included so that you can use them later as a basis for extension work.

> *How to Kick-start a dragon* focuses the children's attention on the **chick**, **bang**, **puff**, and **cross** rhyme families.
>
> A list of rhyme family words is given on p. 85.

Introducing the Story Rhyme

As usual, begin with the Big Book. *How to kick-start a dragon* has a somewhat eccentric rhyme scheme. The story is about Og, a 'Heath Robinson' type of inventor, who builds a dragon out of scrap metal and other bits and pieces. His two child apprentices realise that Og's dragon could save the town from a gang of marauding bandits that have been terrorising everyone. They tell the mayor, and the dragon does save the town because it unexpectedly explodes! Nevertheless, the dragon turns out to be Og's best invention ever, just as he had hoped.

The story is set in 'story book' time; it has a medieval feel to it, even though modern life intervenes in the shape of motor-bike engines and the other paraphernalia used to construct the dragon. When you read through the Story Rhyme for the first time, allow the children to focus on the story as they need to be able to follow the narrative flow. The rhyme pattern can be secondary, although emphasis can be placed on the final line in each verse, as in 'And I'm going to get it right!' Then read through the story again, placing greater emphasis on the rhymes, and using the device of guided response questions – see Story Rhyme 1 (p. 17).

Checking narrative comprehension

■ Why did Og want people to think that he was the best inventor of his day? How did he plan to make them think that?

■ What kind of things did Og use to make his dragon?

■ Did Og's helpers think that he was a good inventor?

■ What does 'gloss' mean? What does 'floss' mean?

■ Why was the mayor looking sick?

and so on.

You can also reinforce the story and the rhyme families by making links with other areas of the curriculum (see ideas at the end of this section).

Links to other ORT stories

The story is reminiscent of the tale of the wooden horse used by the Greeks to fool the people of Troy, and you could bring in this story too. ORT stories with links to the themes in this Story Rhyme include: *The go-kart*, *The snowman*, *The whatsit*, *Vanishing cream*, and *Yasmin and the flood* – all about inventing or solutions to problems.

Developing phonological awareness

Use the reinforcement activities suggested in Story Rhyme 1 (p. 17) to consolidate awareness of the phonological patterns in *How to kick-start a dragon*. Then develop this awareness with work on onsets, rhymes, and analogies.

> Salient onsets linked to *How to kick-start a dragon*
>
> **p   b   cr   ch**

Onset work

The Clue Cards for Story Rhyme 11 allow you to work on two important onsets, 'cr' (cross) and 'ch' (chick). The other Clue Card onsets are 'p' and 'b', which are already familiar (see Story Rhymes 1 and 7).

You can use the Clue Card 'chick' for further work on double-consonant onsets that have a single sound (see also Story Rhymes 6 and 8, for 'sh' and 'kn', pp. 50 and 62). Follow the method described in Story Rhyme 4 (p. 32). Bring in the other single-phoneme double-consonant onsets on the Alphabet

Frieze as well (TH, and WH). Explain that the onsets 'ch', 'sh', 'th', and 'wh' are special, and that is why they all have a special colour of their own on the Alphabet Frieze.

The Clue Card 'cross' can be used to reinforce teaching of the –R onsets encountered in Story Rhyme 10 ('br', 'dr', 'gr'). Follow the suggestions made in Story Rhymes 4, 8, and 9 for teaching and segmenting these onsets (see pp. 39, 62 and 68).

The Clue Cards 'puff' and 'bang' can be used for revision of the onsets 'p' and 'b'. Use the Clue Card method (see Story Rhyme 4, p. 39), and also follow earlier suggestions for these onsets (see SR 1 and SR 7, pp. 17 and 57). You might wish to include the onset 'd' in this oral work, to enable you to work on the confusable letters 'p', 'b', and 'd' together (see Extension activities below).

Reinforcing the onset work

This oral work can then be supplemented in a number of ways. There are two pages in the Alphabet Photocopy Masters that practise 'b', 'p', and 'd' (pp. 2 and 4), and a page for 'ch', 'th', 'wh' and 'sh' (p. 42). These special digraphs also have individual pages (pp. 27 – 30). The 'cr' onset is practised on p. 46. As usual, the Alphabet Frieze, Tabletop Alphabets, and Card Games (Set 1) can also be used as a basis for support activities, and the ideas in the Onset section (p. 94) can be adapted to the onsets in *How to Kick-start a dragon*.

- The children can think of different foods that begin with 'ch'. ('I looked in my lunch box, and I found . . . chips, chocolate, cheese sandwiches, chilli-flavour crisps, etc.')
- The children can make up some alliterative sentences for Biff to practise 'b': 'Biff's balloon went bang!'; 'Biff bounced her ball into the bin'.
- The children can listen to a recording of the song about Puff the Magic Dragon, or you can read them the verses of the song. Then they can think up some adjectives to describe Puff (e.g. poor Puff, peckish Puff), and discuss how Puff differs from Og's dragon.

Extension activities

Link sounds to letters by playing the Clue Game for Onsets (see Story Rhyme 3, p. 32).

Onsets with familiar rimes

CH	chip chat chin chap chop chill chum chuck chug
CR	cram crop crab crag crow crash crack crush cress
Clue Cards	zip cat pin cap shop jam crab bag hill mum duck snow plug flash sack brush dress

Include activities that segment the onset for further consolidation, see Story Rhyme 9 (p. 69).

You can also have a special session on the onsets 'p', 'd', and 'b'. Children often confuse these onsets when using their lower case letters. One way of working on these onsets is via the Clue Game, following the 'shared rime' technique suggested in Story Rhyme 9 (p. 70).

B, D, and P words with the same rimes

big	dig	pig
ban	Dan	pan
Ben	den	pen
bay	day	pay
bill	dill	pill
buck	duck	puck
bid	did	
beg		peg
bop		pop
	dot	pot
bash	dash	
bug	dug	
back		pack
bong		pong
Clue Cards	pig fan pen hay hill duck hid leg shop knot flash plug sack long	

The Clue Game onset work can also be extended by using some of the other activities in the Onset section (p. 94).

Rhyme work

Go through the Story Rhyme again, asking the children to remind you of the rhyming words. Alternatively, you could divide the children into four teams, those that have to spot the 'cross' rhymes, those that have to spot the 'bang' rhymes, those that have to spot the 'puff' rhymes, and those that have to spot the 'chick' rhymes.

Reinforcing the rhyme work

You can build on this work by supplementing it with some of the ideas in the Rhyme section (p. 97). Any of the Card Games in Set 2 can be played, choosing games at an appropriate developmental level. The rhyme activities in the Story Rhyme Photocopy Masters can also be used (those coded 'L' are based on oral recognition of rhyme).

Another way to reinforce this work is to extend the dragon theme to the Onset activities (p. 94).

- The children can make a board game involving a dragon and some robbers (a suitable outline for a board game is provided as a photocopiable resource, p. 119). The robbers are at the start, and the dragon is at the finish. Use a selection of the Rhyme Picture Cards. The children have to pick a card before they throw the dice, say what it is, and say something that rhymes with it. If they get it wrong or can't think of a rhyme, they miss their go. The first robber to reach the dragon is the winner.

- The children can play a 'dragons and robbers' game in the hall or the playground. A few children will be the dragons, the rest will be robbers. Use a selection of Rhyme Picture Cards. Give one of each set to a dragon (e.g. 'ball'). Give the others to the robbers (e.g. have a robber with 'wall', one with 'hall', and one with 'fall'). The dragons have to catch their robbers, by asking the other children if they have a picture that rhymes with their card. The first dragon to round up all of his/her robbers is the winner.

- The children can paint pictures of scenes from the Story Rhyme. These can be stuck onto card, and used as sequencing cards to facilitate the retelling of each rhyme in the correct order.

Extension work

Extend the oral work to rime spellings:

- Play the 'dragons and robbers' chasing game using the Rhyme Word Cards instead of the Rhyme Picture Cards.

- Play the 'dragons and robbers' board game using the Rhyme Word Cards and a wipe board. The children have to spell the rhyming word that they think of on the wipe board before they can

take their turn with the dice.

- Add text to the picture scenes from the Story Rhyme or the other rhymes. The children should provide this text in their best writing.

Other activities at the end of the Rhyme section also involve spelling patterns, and these can also be adapted to the rhymes in *How to kick-start a dragon*. The children can play some of the Card Games in Set 4, and use the Story Rhyme Photocopy Masters for further consolidation and assessment (those coded 'RW' involve writing rimes).

Using analogies

Play the rhyming version of the Clue Game using the Clue Cards 'chick', 'bang', 'puff', and 'cross'. Play the game on separate days for the different families.

The Clue Card 'puff' illustrates an inconsistent pattern. As well as the 'uff' rime (muff, cuff) there is the unusual 'ough' pattern (tough, enough). You can use this as a teaching point when the children nominate inconsistent rimes for 'puff'.

Reinforcing the analogy work

Supplement the Clue Game with other Analogy activities from the Analogy section, adapting them to the rime families in *How to kick-start a dragon*. The Card Games provide further opportunities for consolidation, and there are some analogy activities in the Story Rhyme Photocopy Masters.

- Make a 'roly rhyme maker' for the 'chick' family. Use the onsets CH, QU, TH, BR, PR, TR, CL, and FL. The children have to write each rhyme word in one of two lists, one for single sound onsets (chick, quick, thick), and one for double sound onsets (brick, prick, trick, click, flick). For the first list, they need to think of another word with the same onset and write it by the side of the first (chick–chin). For the second list, they could write another word with the same rime (brick–kick).

- Give the children some old magazines. Ask them to do a word search for the 'chick' family, and to write down the words that they find. Make the search more difficult by asking them to do a second search through the same magazines, this time to find words to match each onset of the words that they found (e.g. thick–thumb, lick–lamp).

Extension work

Extend the Clue Game to bisyllables (see Story Rhyme 5, p. 47). A list of useful words appears on the next page.

Segmenting rime spellings

The Clue Card spellings in Story Rhyme 11 are also complex ones, using two letters to write a single final sound (the -ss in 'cross', the -ff in 'puff', the -ng in 'bang' and the -ck in 'chick'). The Clue Card words 'puff' and 'cross' can be segmented in Story Rhyme 12, which uses the Clue Words 'grass', 'kiss', and 'cliff'.

The Clue Card words 'bang' and 'chick' can be segmented here, following the procedure given in Story Rhyme 9 (p. 68). Refer back to previous Clue Cards using similar consonant digraphs (i.e. 'duck', 'sack', and 'clock' for CK, and 'king' and 'long' for NG).

Long words with familiar rimes

chicken	chick + hen
ticket, cricket, wicket	chick + net
picking	chick + king
lipstick	zip + chick
suffer	puff + her
muffin	puff + pin
crossbar	cross + star
crossbow	cross + snow
hanger, gangster	bang + her
hanging	bang + king
orangutan	o + bang + u + fan

The CH and TCH endings

CH	such much
	munch lunch
	rich
TCH	pitch witch
	match patch
	clutch Dutch
	fetch
	Scotch

Finally, you can use the onset CH as a basis for discussing words that have a 'ch' sound at the *end*. Only some of these represent the 'ch' sound with CH. Others use TCH. However, this 't' does not make a separate sound from 'ch', as shown by the identical pronunciations that we give to words like 'witch' and 'which'.

Explain that we need to remember words use TCH, and which words use CH.

Links with other curriculum areas

'Cross'

Design Technology Create some different patterns with cross-stitch. Provide different sizes of squared material as a base for the children to work on. The children could also make something functional from the material (e.g. simple egg cosies can be stitched from material with a small check, and then decorated with cross-stitch – links also to 'chick').

English/History/Comparative Religion Where do we see crosses? Why do we use crosses in Christian church-yards to mark people's graves? What symbols are used in other religions? (crescent, star of David, sun signs.)

Maths How do you play Noughts and Crosses on a 3×3 grid? Does the game get easier or more difficult if you use 16 squares? What about if you only use 4 squares – can you ever lose? Work out and count the number of winning patterns that you can create for each board size. Is there a bigger pattern that you can pick out?

'Puff'

Art Make pictures with dry-powder paints (see Story Rhyme 1).

Science Which kinds of substance can form puffs? Anything that smokes is an obvious example, but we also have 'puffs' of cloud, and powder 'puffs'. What do all of these have in common? (all are extremely small particles suspended in air). How do we make a dandelion 'puff'? (by blowing on it). What makes us puff? (running too fast). What about puffs of steam? (when liquids are heated).

'Chick'

For activities connected to birds, see 'hen' activities in *The Mungle Flap* (Story Rhyme 3).

'Bang'

An associated theme is **dragon**.

Design Technology Make models of the dragon out of junk or construction kits. How can you make your model move? (see transport ideas in *Supersonic engine juice*, Story Rhyme 1).

English What do you think the robbers felt like when they saw the dragon? What words could you use to describe the dragon?

Music Which instruments do we use to make loud bang-like noises in musical pieces? (cymbals, drums). Experiment with some different rhythms using these instruments. What kinds of effect can we create?

Children can retell the story using sounds to accompany the robbers creeping quietly then running away noisily. Instruments made from metal could be used for the dragon moving and finally going bang. Different instruments and beaters could be investigated. The music can be recorded on a tape recorder or on paper using pictorial symbols.

Alternatively, listen to instruments that you play with a beater like drums. Make a collection of beaters, e.g. wooden, plastic, rubber tipped. Get children to shut their eyes while one child chooses a beater and uses it to play a drum. Others then open their eyes and one child tries to play the drum using the same beater as the first child.

Science You could use the idea of making something look scary to talk about camouflage in nature in general, and about animals changing their appearance for a purpose. For example, the hawk-moth caterpillar mimics a poisonous snake by the markings on its underside, porcupine fish blow themselves up and raise 'spikes' to look like scary porcupines, and the crested rat can make itself look like a skunk by parting its hair. In *The hedgehog* the ORT dog, Floppy, is fooled by a hedgehog curled up like a ball.

Rhyme families in Story Rhyme 11

bang

sang	hanger	boomerang
hang	gangster	overhang
rang	hanging	orangutan
sprang	hangar	
gang		
fang		
slang		
clang		
twang		
pang		

cross

loss	crossword
boss	crossbar
moss	crossroad
Ross	crossbow
toss	crosscut
gloss	across
floss	crisscross
dross	emboss

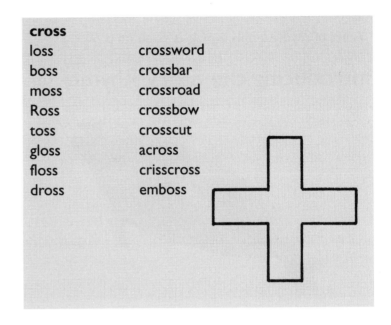

chick

thick	chicken	candlestick
stick	quickly	pickpocket
pick	ticket	
quick	picking	
sick	sticky	
Dick	wicked	
trick	cricket	
brick	ticking	
kick	picket	
Nick	wicket	
lick	Patrick	
click	toothpick	
tick	homesick	
slick	lipstick	
flick	broomstick	
wick		
prick		
nick		
hick		
crick		

puff

stuff	suffer
bluff	fluffy
buff	muffin
cuff	muffler
fluff	buffer
gruff	stuffy
snuff	buffet
duff	handcuff
ruff	snuffbox
huff	
scuff	

NB Some of the words in the lists may be unfamiliar to the children. However, they have been included so that you can use them later as a basis for extension work.

> *My home* focuses the children's attention on the
> **grass**, **kiss**, **stung**, and **cliff** rhyme families.
>
> A list of rhyme family words is given on p. 91.

Introducing the Story Rhyme

My home is about the homes and habitats of different
animals. The rhyme structure is very subtle, and varies
from verse to verse. Some of the rhymes are internal
ones (e.g. 'over *sand, and* . . . ', 'on this *cliff*, where the
stiff winds . . .). *My home* also uses alliteration (shared
beginning sounds) and assonance to create a rich
focus on sounds. Assonance is the repetition of
internal sounds, as in 'green sea', or 'loud shout'. As
you read *My home* for the first time, enunciate slowly,
lingering over repeated sounds and stressing internal
rhymes.

For example, when reading the first verse, linger
over the 's' sounds 'This is my home, said Snake,
with a soft hiss'. The repetition of 's' sounds in the
first verse creates a vivid image of a hissing, slithering snake, so let the sounds paint a picture of the
animal in the children's imaginations.

On repeated readings, allow the children to supply
some of the rhymes, including the internal rhymes
('over sand, and — ?'), or some of the alliterative
words, using guided response questions (see Story
Rhyme 1, p. 17). This is the most 'poem-like' Story
Rhyme, and can be used as a vehicle for thinking
about sounds in words at multiple levels (beginnings, ends, middles).

Checking narrative comprehension

■ Where do snakes live? What is scrub?

■ Why is the grass so dry?

■ What colour is land that is the colour of brass?

■ What is the 'sun's kiss'?

■ Why do snakes like hot places?

■ Are there any snakes in this country? Are they
poisonous?

and so on.

You can also reinforce the story and the rhyme families by making links with other areas of the curriculum (see ideas at the end of this section).

Links to other ORT stories

Many ORT stories focus on the topics 'homes' and
'animals'. You could use: *The hedgehog, A new dog,
The chase, The dolphin pool, House for sale, The new
house, A monster mistake, The pet shop, Pip at the zoo,
Roy and the budgie, Pip and the little monkey*, and all
six titles in the non-fiction Fact Finders series Unit
C, 'Houses and homes'.

Developing phonological awareness

Use the reinforcement activities suggested in Story
Rhyme 1 (p. 17) to consolidate awareness of the
phonological patterns in *My home*. Then develop this
awareness with work on onsets, rhymes, and analogies.

Onset work

> **Salient onsets linked to *My home***
>
> **gr   st   cl   k**

As *My home* has a strong focus on beginning sounds,
it provides an ideal opportunity for more practice in
segmenting onsets.

Read through the story again, asking the children to
tell you which words have similar beginning sounds
in each verse. Some of the similarity is *within* the
onset. For example, in the first verse there are lots of
's' words, but many of these have different onsets
(soft, snake, slide, scrub, etc.). Ask the children to
group the 's' words into those that have the same
beginning sound (said, soft, sand, sun) and those that
do not. Ask them why the ones that do not are different, and which sounds they can hear in those words.

As usual, you can also use the Clue Cards for onset
work, following the suggestions in Story Rhyme 4
(p. 39). The Clue Card for 'grass' can be used to

revise the –R onsets learned in previous Story Rhymes ('dr', 'cr', 'br'). The Clue Card for 'cliff' can be used to revise the –L onsets ('pl', 'fl', 'cl'). Follow the suggestions made in Story Rhyme 9 (p. 69) for segmenting these onsets.

Reinforcing the onset work

This oral work can then be supplemented in a number of ways. There are a few pages in the Alphabet Photocopy Masters that practise the –R onsets (pp. 43, 45, 46 and 50), and p. 47 practises 'cl'. Other –L onsets are practised on pp. 44 ('fl') and 48 ('gl', 'bl', 'sl'). As usual, the Alphabet Frieze, Tabletop Alphabets and Card Games (Set 1) can all be used as a basis for support activities, and the ideas in the Onset section (p. 94) can be adapted to the onsets in *My home*.

- The children can think of some more ways for the characters in each verse to go home. The *sliding* snake might *slip* and *slither* his way home. The high-flying gull might *drift* and *dream* his way home, *drowsing* on the cross-wind. The *snarling* bear might *snap* and *sneer* his way home, *snacking* on *snowberries*.

- The children can think of alliterative descriptions of the habitats where the different animals live. The snake's desert might be *dry* and *dreary*. The gull's cliff might be *steep* and *stony*.

- The children can think of some adjectives to describe their own homes, using 'h'. 'A *happy* home, a *healthy* home, a *hungry* home.'

Extension activities

Link sounds to letters:

- Ask the children which letters they would need to write the sounds at the beginning of the different descriptions of the animals' homes or actions. Which letters would we need to start writing *slip* and *slither*? Which sounds can you hear at the beginning, if you say the words nice and slowly? Which letters would we need to start writing *dry* and *dreary*?

- Play the Clue Game for Onsets (see Story Rhyme 3, p. 32).

All of these Clue Card onsets have been met before. However, the children can now use them in more words, and repetition provides useful consolidation work.

- Segment the onset (see Story Rhyme 9, p. 69)

The Clue Game onset work can also be extended by using some of the other activities in the Onset section (p. 94).

Onsets with familiar rimes

CL clan clip club clog clap clam clop clot cluck clash cling

ST stub stun stay stop stab stag stuck still stall star stow stash sting stock stack stick stuff

GR gran grip grub grin grog grit grid grab grim grill grow

Clue Cards zip fan tub dog lid cap sun hit jam hay shop crab swim knot bag hill mum duck ball star snow plug flash king clock sack chick puff

Rhyme work

Read the Story Rhyme to the children again, emphasising the rich sound patterns, and letting them supply the rhymes.

Supplement this work by looking at other poems about animals and their habitats, or by helping the children to make up their own. What words would we need for a poem about where a snail or a mole or an ant lived? In each case, let the children think of words that describe these animals and where they live, and words that rhyme with them. The rhymes can be internal rhymes, just like in *My home*.

For example, a snail lives in its shell. The shell is like its house – so does it need a bell? Snails leave silvery trails. Where might these trails be left? Over nails? On pails? Moles live in holes. Where do they dig their holes? (in gardens, parks). What are the holes like? (dark, den), and so on.

Reinforcing the rhyme work

As usual, any of the ideas in the Rhyme section (p. 97) can be adapted to the rhymes used in *My home*. Similarly, any of the Card Games in Set 2 can be played, choosing games at an appropriate developmental level. The rhyme activities in the Story Rhyme Photocopy Masters can also be used (those coded 'L' are based on oral recognition of rhyme).

Another way to reinforce this work is to adapt the Rhyme activities by extending the 'home' theme:

- Use a selection of Rhyme Picture Cards, none of which rhyme with each other, to play the racing game. Place the cards face-up at the end of a hall. Pairs of children take it in turns to race and find the card which rhymes with a word called by the teacher or another child. The first one to find the rhyme is 'home'.

- Use a selection of Rhyme Picture Cards and create a simple board game with a start and finish (a board game outline is provided as a photocopiable resource, see p. 119). The finish is 'home'. The aim is to be first home, by throwing a dice to move along the board. Before moving, each player takes a Rhyme Picture Card from a pile and says what the word is and something which rhymes with it. If they are unable to think of a rhyme or get it wrong, they miss their go.

- The children can play 'Happy Families' with the Rhyme Picture Cards. For four players, you will need eight rhyme families. Shuffle the cards, and share them between the players. The aim is to get a complete family of rhymes, by requesting specific cards when it is your turn. For example, if you have the pictures 'star' and 'bar' from the 'star' family, then you can ask someone if they have a picture that rhymes with 'star'. If the person that you ask has the rhyme that you need, they have to give it to you, and you get another turn. If not, they can ask you for a card. The first player to collect two complete rhyming sets is the winner.

Extension work

Extend the oral work to rime spellings:

- The children can play the 'racing' game with Rhyme Word Cards instead of with Rhyme Picture Cards.

- The children can play the 'First Home' board game with the Rhyme Word Cards instead of with Rhyme Picture Cards. Each player has to spell the rhyme that they think of on a wipe-board before they can take their turn. If they are wrong, they miss a turn.

- The children can play 'Happy Families' with the Rhyme Word Cards instead of with the Rhyme Picture Cards.

Other activities at the end of the Rhyme section also involve spelling patterns, and these can also be adapted to the rhymes in *My home*. The children can play some of the Card Games in Set 4, and use the Story Rhyme Photocopy Masters for further consolidation and assessment (those coded 'RW' involve writing rimes).

Using analogies

Play the rhyming version of the Clue Game using the Clue Cards for 'grass', 'stung', 'kiss', and 'cliff'.

Reinforcing the analogy work

Supplement the Clue Game with other Analogy activities from the Analogy section (p. 99), adapting them to the rime families in *My home*. The Card Games provide further opportunities for consolidation, and there are some Analogy activities in the Story Rhyme Photocopy Masters.

- Photocopy or copy out different verses of *My home*, leaving gaps for the rhyme family words, including in the middle of lines (the internal rhymes). The children have to write the correct words in the gaps, using the Clue Cards and the Alphabet Frieze to help them.

- Make a 'roly rhyme maker' for the 'stung' family (see p. 27). Use the onsets H, S, SW, FL, CL, L, R. The children have to write the words that they can make with the roller across the top of a piece of paper, and then add a rhyming word underneath each word by either adding to the onset (stung, slung, sprung) or subtracting from the onset (sung, lung, rung).

Extension Work

As these clue words have few familiar multisyllabic neighbours, concentrate on extending this work by segmenting the rime.

Use the method for segmenting the Clue Card spellings given in Story Rhyme 9 (p. 69). Relate the spellings back to previous Clue Cards using similar consonant digraphs. For 'stung', these are 'king', 'long', and 'bang', for 'kiss' these are 'dress' and 'cross', and for 'cliff' there is 'puff'.

The final consonant digraph SS is special, because when it is paired with A, the vowel changes its sound in some dialects. Discuss this with the children if it is appropriate. You can use the discussion to think about the sounds that the different vowels make when they are on their own. Of course, you can still have this discussion for consistent dialects!

You can also extend this work by asking the children

which other letters can come twice at the end of English words. The others are FF, LL, and ZZ. Encourage the children to think about how the vowel sounds change in different rimes. **NB** The 'u' rimes ending in LL are usually pronounced to rhyme with 'bull', but have a set of exceptions which rhyme with 'dull' (gull, hull, mull and null).

Rimes which end in the same double consonant				
FF		stiff		stuff
LL	wall	fell	pill	full/gull
SS	class	cress	miss	toss	fuss
ZZ	jazz			fuzz
Clue Cards	bell	hill	ball	dress	cross
		puff	grass	cliff	kiss

There is also a special page in the Alphabet Photocopy Masters for working on vowel sounds (p. 37).The Analogy activities (p. 99) can also be adapted to support rime segmentation and vowel work.

/ The children can make a 'word ladder'. The first word must have a – SS rime, for example, 'miss'. The next step in the ladder must change the vowel – 'moss'. The next step can change the onset – 'loss'. The next step can change the vowel – 'lass'. See who can make the longest ladder by choosing the best words, always alternately changing the onset and the vowel. Do the same for the other consonant digraphs covered in Story Rhymes 9–12 (-SH, -NG, -CK, -FF, -LL).

/ The children can make a more complicated word ladder by changing the final consonants as well as the onsets and vowels. Single final consonants must be included, in order to give enough words. The steps on the ladder are: change vowel, change onset, change final consonant/s. For example, 'miss' – 'mess' – 'less' – 'let' – 'lot' – 'pot' – 'pong' etc.

Links with other curriculum areas

'Grass'

Design Technology How can we make a grass skirt? Do we need to dry the grass first? Then what? What other clothes can we make out of grass?

Science Grow some seeds, e.g. grass seed, mustard and cress. What do seeds need to grow? Try putting some seeds in a dark position and some in a light position. Which grow tallest? But which grow most healthy and green? Perform an experiment to find out if the seeds need water by watering one lot of seeds but not another. Keep a diary recording what happens to the seeds.

'Cliff'

History Why did many kings build castles at the tops of cliffs, looking out to sea (an example is Dover Castle). What other buildings do we often find on cliffs? (lighthouses). Why?

Science What kinds of birds nest in cliffs (e.g. puffins, gannets)? Are cliffs safe places to build nests? What are the advantages and the disadvantages?

Science/Geography Look at photographs (e.g. postcards) showing cliffs. What colour are the rocks? Ask the children to bring in any rocks or pebbles they have found by the sea. What do they look/feel like? Why are some rough and some smooth? Provide the children with different sorts of rocks so they can discover which are hard and which are soft by seeing which will scratch another rock (hard rocks scratch soft rocks).

'Stung'

Science/English Use information books to find out which insects sting. All true insects have six legs. Sort the pictures according to how many legs they have, to eliminate e.g. spiders, centipedes. (This will help to develop the important skill of scientific classification.) Make annotated diagrams showing the attributes of various stinging insects.

'Kiss'

Maths **hiss** Play a snake game. Cut string into different lengths, either longer or shorter than 10cm. Give each child a card snake 10cm long. Mix the string snakes up and put in a pile. Each player takes a turn to take a piece of string. Half aim to pick one shorter than their card, half aim for longer. They measure each choice against the card and only keep it if is the correct length. If the string is the correct length, they could indicate a 'score' by making a snake's hissing sound. The winner is the first to an agreed number of snakes.

'Home'

Art Make a camouflage picture by using the same crayons or paint to create a background, and to make two cut-out animals. Stick one of the animals on the background that is made out of the same materials, and one on another background. Which animal is well camouflaged?

English What is your home like? What do you like about your home? How do you feel when you are at home? Would you like to be home alone? Do the people in your home make it feel good?

Geography Look at houses built in hot countries. What are they made of? Do they have large or small windows? Why? What are the rooms shaped like? Make model houses from junk materials.

History Look at pictures of homes from the past. How are they different? Where did people wash/cook? How did they heat/light their homes?

Maths Do some class surveys about homes. How many windows at the front of your house? How many people have a fireplace in the living-room? What colour is your front door? What is the roof/door made of? Record the results on Venn diagrams or graphs.

Science Where do different animals live? Why do they live there? Are they safe/near food/well camouflaged?

Rhyme families in Story Rhyme 12

grass

class	classroom	grasshopper
glass	passport	underpass
pass	classmate	embarass
mass	grassland	encompass
brass	eyeglass	
bass	bypass	
ass	hourglass	
lass	surpass	
crass		

cliff

stiff	sheriff
sniff	tariff
skiff	bailiff
whiff	midriff
	plaintiff

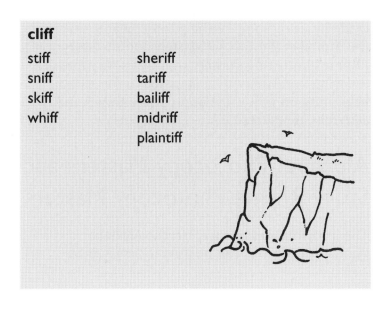

stung

hung
sung
swung
flung
clung
lung
rung
strung
slung
sprung
wrung
dung

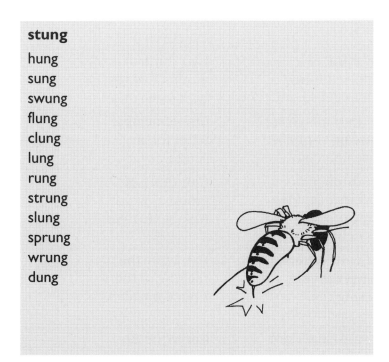

kiss

miss
Swiss
hiss
bliss

NB Some of the words in the lists may be unfamiliar to the children. However, they have been included so that you can use them later as a basis for extension work.

Progression and assessment

In order to assess children's learning progress, a Checklist of Phonological Skills and a progression sheet for Rhyme and Analogy Skills are provided here. However, additional assessment tools can be made by using some of the photocopiable sheets in the Alphabet Photocopy Masters and the Story Rhyme Photocopy Masters, and by using some of the games and activities suggested in the section beginning on p. 94. The appropriate games and activities are marked AA.

Alphabet Photocopy Masters and Story Rhyme Photocopy Masters

The individual letter sheets in the Alphabet Photocopy Masters can be used to assess letter learning, and the sheets on pp. 31 – 39 enable assessment of groups of individual letters.

The activities on p. 52 and pp. 56 – 61 assess knowledge of the entire alphabet. The activities on the other pages assess knowledge of different blends and digraphs, and are referred to in the teaching notes for the individual Story Rhymes.

Some of the sheets in the Story Rhyme Photocopy Masters can also be used to assess knowledge of the rhyme families introduced by each story and are marked to indicate whether they assess the child's oral rhyme knowledge (listening), reading and recognising, or writing and spelling ability. See the introductory teaching notes at the beginning of the book.

Progression in Rhyme and Analogy skills

Skill	Level 1 Guided	Level 2 Supported	Level 3 Independent
	Can recognise.	Can generate.	Can use effectively.
Onset 1 (oral)	Can isolate sound correctly in word supplied by teacher.	Can think of a word beginning with target sound.	Can think of group of words with same onset.
Onset 2 (letters)	Can find match for sound on Alphabet Frieze with help.	Can find match for sound on Alphabet Frieze unaided.	Can remember letter for any sound.
Rhyme 1 (oral)	Can recognise whether two words supplied by teacher rhyme.	Can think of a word that rhymes with word supplied by teacher.	Can think of group of words with same rhymes.
Rhyme 2 (letters)	Can recognise spelling pattern of target rhyme on Word Tree.	Can write letters in target rhyme by using the Clue Card.	Can write the spelling of the rhyme unaided.
Analogy	Can recognise spelling pattern of target rhyme on Word Tree and of target onset on Alphabet Frieze	Can use Clue Card and Alphabet Frieze to make an analogy with teacher's help.	Can write the spellings of analogous words unaided, using Clue Cards and Alphabet Frieze.

Checklist of phonological skills

Name _____ **Date** _____

	Can recognise with help.	Can write with support from Alphabet Frieze and Word Tree.	Can spell independ-ently.
ONSETS			
1 Single phoneme onsets			
2 CH, SH, TH, WH, KN			
3 Double phoneme onsets			
RHYMES			
1 Simple CVC rhymes			
2 Complex CVCC rhymes			
ANALOGIES			
1 With CVC words			
2 With CCVC words			
3 With CVCC words			
4 With CCVCC words			

Note C = Consonant, V = Vowel. CVC clue word = 'zip'; CCVC clue word = 'crab'; CVCC clue word = 'bell'; CCVCC clue word = 'flash'.

Activities and games to support the Story Rhymes

A wide range of different activities and games can be used to support the work on spelling, sound, and analogy that arises from the Story Rhymes. These activities and games can be divided into activities that support onset awareness, activities that support rhyme awareness, and activities that help with analogies. For each Story Rhyme, the teaching sequence should be

- onset
- rhyme
- analogy

Within the onset, rhyme, and analogy sections, some of the activities have been designed to develop sound awareness, while others have been designed to help children to link sounds to letters. The sound-based activities are listed first in each section, and are marked with a listening symbol (👂). The activities that have been designed to link sounds to letters are listed next, and are marked with a writing symbol (✏️). The usual developmental sequence is to begin with oral activities, and then to progress to writing:

- begin by becoming a good listener (👂)
- then learn to link letters to sounds (✏️)

However, some children may be able to cope with the writing activities from the first Story Rhyme. These children will probably already have good phonological awareness skills, and can begin with the writing activities (✏️). Other children may continue to need oral practice with sounds on every Story Rhyme. A child who takes more time to become phonologically aware can be given continued practice at the oral level with the listening activities (👂). For any Story Rhyme, you can teach at both of these phonological levels, simply by giving some children listening activities (👂), and others writing activities (✏️).

Links with the Rhyme and Analogy Card Games

Many of the activities and games suggested here use the Rhyme and Analogy Card Game cards. There are two kinds of playing card, cards with pictures and cards with print.

The *picture* cards support either onset activities or rhyme activities. The onset cards are the Sound Picture Cards, which introduce the children to initial letter sounds. The rhyme cards are the Rhyme Picture cards, which introduce the children to rhyming sounds.

The cards with *print* also support either onset or rhyme activities. The Letter Cards can be used with the Sound Picture Cards to link sound to spelling, or on their own to develop letter-name knowledge. The Letter Cards can also be used on their own to develop visual letter-discrimination skills, particularly of visually confusing letters such as b, d, and p. In addition, the Letter Cards can be used to support other phonic or handwriting programmes in use in the classroom.

The Rhyme Word Cards can be used with the Rhyme Picture cards to link sound to spelling. They can also be used for analogy activities. See also the notes for the teacher supplied with the Card Games, and written by Dr Clare Kirtley.

Rhyme and Analogy Card Game Cards

Cards with Pictures

- Sound Picture Cards – teach initial sounds
- Rhyme Picture Cards – teach rhyming sounds

Cards with Print

- Letter Cards – teach letters for initial sounds
- Rhyme Word Cards – teach rhyming spellings

Onset activities

The overall goal of the onset activities is for the children to become familiar with the whole alphabet. They should:

- Know the most frequent sound made by each of the alphabet letters at the beginning of words.
- Know the sounds made by the consonant digraphs 'ch', 'sh', 'th' and 'wh'.

The order of presentation of each letter sound, and thus progression through the alphabet, is flexible. The activities can be adapted for different Story Rhymes. To demonstrate how to do this, some of the activities have already been adapted to each

Story Rhyme. For these activities, the corresponding Story Rhyme is marked (**SR1**, **SR2**, etc.). These relate to the list below. Activities that can be used for assessment purposes are marked **AA**.

SR1	*Supersonic engine juice*
SR2	*Scat, cat!*
SR3	*The Mungle Flap*
SR4	*Bad day, good day*
SR5	*Who wants to play with a troll?*
SR6	*The Spell Shell*
SR7	*That's nothing!*
SR8	*Rockpool rap*
SR9	*The King's socks*
SR10	*Gran, Gran!*
SR11	*How to kick-start a dragon*
SR12	*My home*

Listening activities

Encourage children to say tongue twisters, and to make up their own. Then display the children's tongue twisters, for example by writing them onto long tongues, and sticking them onto children's pictures of faces. **SR2, SR5, SR6.**

Ask the children to think of adjectives that begin with the same sound as their name, or characters from stories, e.g. Wonderful Wilma. **SR1, SR4, SR6, SR7.**

Ask the children to make up alliterative sentences involving their names, or the names of animals, e.g. A baby baboon in a big balloon; Adam likes alligators. Write the sentences in a book and get the children to illustrate them. **SR3, SR4, SR6, SR8, SR9, SR10.**

Play 'I spy' and versions of it, e.g. 'Can you think of something beginning with . . .' ,or 'I'm thinking of something beginning with . . . '. 'We went shopping and bought something beginning with . . . .' **SR7, SR8.**

Children make a display of objects and pictures beginning with a letter. They can sort through a selection of the Sound Picture Cards to find the pictures which begin with the same letter, and add them to the display. **SR1, SR2, SR7.**

Read alliterative poems and stories.

Play 'Add a word game'. Children take it in turns to add a word that begins with the same sound, e.g. I went to the seaside and I took with me, sunglasses, socks, and sandals. **SR1, SR2, SR3, SR4, SR9, SR10.**

Play 'Add an adjective game'. Children take it in turns to add an adjective that begins with the same sound, e.g. I saw five fierce foxes. **SR5.**

Linking sounds to letters

Have a letter of the week. Children make the letter out of plasticine, wool, string, clay. They can use different media to write the letter, e.g. fat and thin felt-tip pens, paint, tracing it in sand. They can make models and pictures of things beginning with the letter. **SR1.**

Write a letter on the door of the classroom or homebay. Children have to say a word which begins with that letter before they go through. **SR2, SR3, SR8.**

Cut out large lower-case letters from sugar paper. Give the children one letter each, and some old magazines. The children have to cut out pictures that begin with the same letter as their large letter, and stick these onto the sugar paper. **SR8.**

Make a book about a letter. For example Biff begins with b. Balloon begins with b. Bicycle begins with b. **SR1, SR3, SR6, SR7.**

Use a selection of the Sound Picture Cards, including all four pictures for the sound being introduced and practised. Ask the children to find all the cards that begin with the same sound, e.g. 'Find all the cards that begin with the same as **m**ouse' or 'find all the cards that begin with **m**'. The cards can be placed on an outline or a picture of something beginning with the sound, e.g. a mouse, or a piece of card with one of the Sound Picture Cards beginning with the sound already placed on it. **SR1.**

Alternatively, the cards can be posted in a box with the letter written on the front. **AA SR2.**

Alternatively, you can introduce a hand puppet whose name begins with the sound being practised (such as the Oxford Reading Tree Character Puppets). Ask the children to use the puppet to sort the Sound Picture Cards for ones that she likes because they begin with the same sound as her name. **SR1.**

Practising lots of letter-sounds together

Children make an alphabet frieze related to a topic such as food or transport, or to their class topic. **SR1**.

Children take turns to trace a letter in the air. Others have to say what the letter is and something which begins with that letter. This could also be used as a movement game in PE. **SR2**.

Present the children with selections of four Sound Picture Cards which all begin with the same sound and one card which begins with a different sound (e.g. ladder, lion, leaf, jug, lamp). Ask the children to find all the pictures that sound the same, and to explain their selection. **AA SR5**.

Present the children with selections of four Letter Cards which all have the same letter on them and one which has a different letter. Ask the children to find all the letters that are the same and then to give the sound and name of the common letter. The children can then be encouraged to think of things which begin with that letter sound. **AA**. *This activity can be used to assess children's letter-discrimination ability, particularly using visually similar letters like p, b, and d.*

Use a selection of the Sound Picture Cards. Sit the children in a circle and spread the cards face-down in the centre. Children take turns to pick a card and say what sound the picture begins with.

Alternatively, a selection of Letter Cards can be used and the children have to pick a card and say what sound the letter makes and something which begins with that letter. If one card for each letter of the alphabet is used, in either version of this activity, the children can each keep their card and at the end line up in alphabetical order.

Use a selection of the Sound Picture Cards. Sit the children in a circle and spread the cards face-up in the centre. Trace a letter with your finger on the back of each child in turn. The child has to find a picture which begins with the letter traced on their back. **SR7**.

Use a selection of the Sound Picture Cards each beginning with a different sound. Place the cards face-up at the end of a hall. Pairs of children take turns to race and find the card beginning with the sound called by the teacher or another child. **SR12** (for rhymes).

Alternatively, a selection of Letter Cards can be used and the children have to find the letter which is at the beginning of the word called by the teacher.

Use a selection of pairs of Sound Picture Cards which begin with the same sound. Each child is given a card, looks at it to see what sound it begins with, then holds it to their chest so that no one else can see it. When the teacher says 'Find your partner', children ask each other 'Do you have a picture beginning with . . . ?'. The children sit down when they find their partner.

Alternatively, you could try to play this activity in silence, with the children showing their cards to each other. The pairs of cards could consist of Sound Picture Cards, or of a Sound Picture Card and a matching Letter Card.

Play Bingo. Use a selection of the Sound Picture Cards, each beginning with a different sound and counters. Make Bingo boards with matching letters written on them (a Bingo board outline is provided as a photocopiable resource, which can be enlarged, see p. 117). The Sound Picture Cards are placed in a box and players take turns to pick out a card. If players have the letter on their board which is the beginning sound of the picture on the card, then they put a counter over that letter. The winner is the first to cover all the letters on their board.

Alternatively, Bingo boards can be made by placing a selection of the Sound Picture Cards on blank grids and placing matching Letter Cards in the box. Or by using the alphabet strips (p. 114) cut up into counters with the Alphabet Mats.

Use a selection of the Sound Picture Cards and a Snakes and Ladders board (a Snakes and Ladders board is provided as a photocopiable resource, which can be enlarged, see pp. 120 – 1). Play as for Snakes and Ladders. You can only go if you correctly say what sound the picture begins with.

Alternatively, the Letter Cards can be used and the player has to give the sound (or sound and letter name) of the letter and something which begins with that letter before climbing the ladder. **SR7, SR12**.

Use a selection of the Sound Picture Cards and a board game with a start and finish (board games are provided as photocopiable resources, see pp. 118 – 9). Throw a dice to move along the board or up the tree, but before moving, each player takes a Sound Picture Card from a pile and says what sound the picture begins with, or 'read' the picture added to the space. If they are unable to give the sound, or get it wrong, they miss their go.

■ Alternatively, the Letter Cards can be used, or letters drawn onto the board, and the player has to give the sound (or sound and letter name) of the letter and something which begins with that letter.

✎ Use all four Sound Picture Cards for each letter of the alphabet, and four strips of paper with twenty-six squares in a row (an alphabet strip is provided as a photocopiable resource, see p. 114). Each of four (or fewer) children is given their own blank alphabet strip. They take it in turns to pick a Sound Picture Card from the pile and write the letter which begins the name of the picture in the right place on their alphabet strip. Cards are returned to the pile. A completed alphabet strip should be available to help children. **AA.** *If used as an assessment activity, the strip can be kept as a record of each child's performance.*

✎ Use all four pictures for the sounds being practised from the Sound Picture Cards. Ask the children to sort all the cards according to their beginning sound, e.g. 'Find all the cards which begin with the same sound'. Cards which begin with the same sound can be placed on an outline or picture of something beginning with that sound or a piece of card with one of the Sound Picture Cards beginning with that sound already placed on it.

■ Alternatively the cards can be posted in boxes with the appropriate letters written on the front. **AA.**

Rhyme activities

The overall goal of the rhyme activities is for the children to become skilled at recognising rhyme and at categorising words by rhyme. Rhyme categories, or rhyme families, should eventually be recognised by shared sound and by shared spelling. The children should be able to:

■ Tell you if one word rhymes with another.

■ Think of a rhyme for a word that you give them.

■ Recognise and match rhyming spellings.

The order of presentation of each rhyme family is determined by the sequence in the Story Rhymes. However, all of the activities can be adapted to each Story Rhyme, and general practice with rhymes that are not in the Story Rhymes will also be beneficial. To demonstrate how to use the different activities with maximum flexibility, some have already been adapted to each Story Rhyme. For these activities, the corresponding Story Rhymes are marked (**SR1**, **SR2**, etc.). Activities that can be used for assessment purposes are marked **AA**.

General listening activities

◖ Read, say, and sing nursery rhymes, rhyming poems and stories. Stop before the rhyming words and encourage children to provide them. Change some of the rhyming words and get the children to correct you. Ask the children to wave every time they hear a word that rhymes with a given word. **SR2**.

◖ Children can record some of their favourite nursery or other rhymes on to cassette. **SR11**.

◖ Children can act out their favourite rhymes or use puppets. **SR11**.

◖ Children make a book containing favourite rhymes and illustrate it. **SR11**.

◖ Clap a rhyme and ask the children to guess which one it is.

◖ Children learn number rhymes and use them to make a number frieze or counting book.

◖ Play 'Add a rhyme game'. Children take turns to add a word that rhymes, e.g. 'On my way to school I saw a dog, a frog and a log'.

◖ Encourage the children to make up rhyming sentences involving their names, names of their family, or animals, e.g. 'My mum likes to hum', 'My mouse loves our house'. **SR2**.

◖ Children make a rhyming display of objects and pictures. They can sort through a selection of the Rhyme Picture Cards to find pictures to add to the display. **SR5**.

◖ Put a Rhyme Picture Card by the door of the classroom or homebay. Children have to say a word which rhymes with the picture before they go through. **SR1**.

◖ Play rhyming 'I spy' and versions of it. For example 'Can you think of something which rhymes with . . . ?' or 'I'm thinking of something which rhymes with . . . ' or 'We went shopping and bought something which rhymes with . . . '. **SR1**.

Put objects into a feely bag. Children take turns to pull out an object and say something that rhymes with it. **SR1.**

Practising the rhyme families in the Story Rhymes

The children can paint pictures of scenes from the Story Rhyme. These can be stuck onto card, and used as sequencing cards to facilitate retelling of the story in the correct order. **SR11.**

The children could make a film strip of the story on a long strip of paper. This can then be wound onto a cardboard tube, with a second cardboard tube providing an anchor for the right-hand end. A 'screen' can then be created by cutting a hole in a box, and the film can be wound across the gap. The frames in the story should appear one-by-one in the hole in the box, before they are wound onto the second tube. The story needs to start at the right-hand end of the strip.

Alternatively, the pictures could be drawn on a strip of card which is pulled across a viewing square cut in another piece of card. The strip is kept in place by threading it through more strips of card, attached at right angles to either side of the viewing square.

Children can mime, act out, dance, or use puppets to retell the Story Rhymes. **SR4.**

Play 'rhyming Kim's game'. Place rhyming objects or a selection of Rhyming Picture Cards or a selection of Rhyming Word Cards on a tray. Ask the children to study them, and then remove one. The children have to say which one is missing. **SR9.**

Use a selection of the Rhyme Picture Cards. Ask the children to find all the cards that rhyme with a particular word. For example 'Find all the cards which rhyme with fan'. The cards can be placed on an outline or picture of one of the rhyming words e.g. a van, or a piece of card with one of the Rhyme Picture Cards already placed on it. **SR1, SR6.**

Alternatively, the cards can be posted in a box with one of the rhyme pictures and/or words on the front. **AA.**

Use a selection of the Rhyme Picture Cards. Introduce a hand puppet whose name rhymes with the rhyme family that you want to practise. Children use the puppet to sort the cards for ones she likes because they rhyme with her name. **SR9.**

Present the children with selections of four Rhyme Picture Cards which rhyme and one card which does not (e.g. men, car, pen, ten, hen). Ask the children to find all the pictures that sound the same and to explain their selection. **AA SR3.**

Use a selection of Rhyme Picture Cards. Sit the children in a circle and spread the cards face-down in the centre. Children take turns to pick a card and say what the picture is and something that rhymes with the picture. **SR2, SR3, SR9.**

Use a selection of Rhyme Picture Cards. Sit the children in a circle and spread the cards face-up in the centre. Say a word to each child in turn and ask them to find a picture which rhymes with that word. **SR2.**

Use a selection of Rhyme Picture Cards, none of which rhyme with each other. Place the cards face-up at the end of a hall. Pairs of children take turns to race and find the card which rhymes with the word called by the teacher or another child. **SR10.**

Alternatively, a selection of Rhyme Word Cards can be used for a more difficult version of this activity.

Use a selection of pairs of Rhyme Picture Cards which rhyme with each other. Each child is given a card, looks at it and then holds it to their chest so that no one else can see it. When the teacher says 'Find your partner', children ask each other 'Do you have a picture which rhymes with.. . .'. The children sit down when they find their partner. **SR3, SR11.**

Alternatively, you could try to play this activity in silence, with the children showing their cards to each other.

Alternatively, a selection of Rhyme Word Cards can be used for a more difficult version of this activity.

Play Bingo. Use a selection of pairs of Rhyme Picture Cards and counters. Make the Bingo boards (see p. 117) by placing one of each pair on blank grids. The remaining cards are placed in a box and players take turns to pick out a card. If players have the picture card on their board which rhymes with the picture on the card chosen, then they put a counter over that picture. The winner is the first to cover all the pictures on their board. **SR3, SR6, SR9.**

Alternatively, a harder version of this game is to write matching rhyme words on the Bingo boards.

Use a selection of Rhyme Picture Cards and a simple board game with a start and finish (see p. 119). Throw a dice to move along the board but before moving, each player takes a Rhyme Picture Card from a pile and says what the picture is and something which rhymes with it. If they are unable to think of a rhyme or get it wrong they miss their go. **SR6, SR11**.

Alternatively, the Rhyme Word Cards can be used for a more difficult game and the children can be encouraged to have a go at spelling the rhyming word they have just thought of on a chalk board, wipe board or in a sand tray. They should be encouraged to use the spelling pattern of the rhyme word on the card they have chosen to help them. **SR6**.

Or you can write your own choice of words on the board game outline on p. 118, with children moving on if they are able to read the word, or write a rhyming word.

It is important to remember that not all rhyming words share the same spelling pattern. If a child thinks of an inconsistent rhyme, use this as an opportunity to talk about exceptions (e.g. the spelling pattern of the word 'sun' may be used to spell the rhyming word 'one', resulting in the incorrect spelling 'wun').

Analogy activities

The overall goal of the analogy activities is for the children to become skilled at linking spelling (rimes) to sound (rhymes). They should be able to recognise that shared sounds can be used as a basis for making predictions about shared spellings. The children should be able to:

■ Group words by rhyme, both by sound and by spelling pattern.

■ Use the spelling pattern of one word as a basis for reading a rhyming word (reading analogies).

■ Use the sound of one word as a basis for spelling a rhyming word (spelling analogies).

Again, the analogy sequence is determined by the sequence of rhyme families in the Story Rhymes. However, all of the activities can be adapted to each Story Rhyme, and general practice with analogies is also useful. A selection of activities have again been adapted for each Story Rhyme, to demonstrate how to use the activities flexibly. The corresponding Story Rhymes are marked after the activity (**SR1**, **SR2**, etc.). Activities that can be used for assessment purposes are marked **AA**.

General analogy activities

Children can create a frieze or individual picture representing any of the storylines using e.g. paint, sponge printing, printing with everyday objects, hand and finger prints, oil pastels, collage of crayon rubbings, collage using natural materials e.g. leaves, pressed flowers, bark, collage using scraps of materia, different coloured paper, or string. This art work can be used as the backdrop to displaying families of rhyming words. **SR3, SR5, SR11**.

The children could copy the words for the frieze from the Clue Cards. If their writing is difficult to read, the teacher can write the words in pencil, and the children can copy over the top or underneath in felt-tip pen. **SR5**.

Rhyming words can be displayed as part of a mobile, as labels attached to 3-D objects. Characters and props from the stories can be made from card, plasticine, salt dough, clay, papier mâché, junk, construction kits. **SR1**.

The teacher can copy parts of the text and get the children to read and order the text, adding their own illustrations. The teacher can cover parts of the recreated text with Post-it notes, and the children can provide the missing words verbally, or by finding the correct word from among other words written on cards, or by writing the word. **SR4, SR7**.

Children can write/draw and tell reviews of the story. They can make little books and class books about the story characters or events. They can create alternative story endings. **SR4, SR5**.

Practising the rhyme families in the Story Rhymes

Make 'flip' books (a flip book is provided as a photocopiable resource, see p. 115). Write the shared spelling pattern of one rhyming family on the last page of the book and the onset of the rhyming family words on shorter pages in front. By turning the pages, new rhyming words are made. If the children forget the new words, they could draw little pictures of the words made by each onset on the back of the onset flaps, as a memory prompt. **SR1, SR3, SR10**.

Make 'word wheels' (a word wheel is provided as a photocopiable resource, see p. 116). Write the shared spelling pattern of one rhyming family on a strip of card and the onset of the rhyming family words on the edge of a circle. Fix the strip behind the circle so that the spelling pattern shows, using a butterfly clip. By turning the strip round, new rhyming words are made. **SR1, SR8.**

Make 'roly rhyme makers'. Use two cardboard tubes, one should be shorter and fit over the top of the other. Write the shared spelling pattern of one rhyming family on the larger tube and the onset of the rhyming family words on the shorter tube. Fit the shorter tube over the longer tube so that by turning the shorter tube round, new rhyming words are made. **SR2, SR11.**

Make some simple jigsaws for the rhyming families (a jigsaw outline is provided as a photocopiable resource, see p. 122). Put the Clue Cards into the centre of rectangular pieces of card, and write some family words into spaces around the centrepoint, cutting out irregular shapes around each family word. The whole card should be used up by creating six or seven large pieces. Jumble three or four jigsaws together, and ask the children to sort out the different pieces and make up the jigsaws. **SR3.**

Create wordsearches involving families of rhyming words. A wordsearch base is provided as a photocopiable resource, see p. 123. **SR4.**

Photocopy a piece of text, and ask the children to use a highlighter to mark all the words that rhyme with a word you write down for them.

Ask the children to make their own Clue Cards for words that rhyme with the Clue Cards on the Word Tree. Ask the children to produce a spelling and a small picture icon, just as on the Clue Cards. Hang these new clue cards onto the Word Tree. Each family of words can be strung together and suspended beneath the appropriate Clue Card, so that all of the spellings are clearly visible. **SR1, SR5.**

■ Alternatively, the children could create Clue Cards in which the picture icon is concealed under a small flap. The picture prompt could be used as a memory prompt only if the children forget the words.

Use the class computer. Type a given rime pattern onto the computer, and ask the children to add different onsets to make rhyme family words. The onsets can be displayed at the bottom of the screen to be selected one at a time. For a more difficult version of the game, omit the onsets – the chidren now add the onsets on their own. This activity can also be adapted to concept keyboards. Type text into the computer leaving blanks where rhymes occur. The children use the concept keyboard, words at the bottom of the screen, or story books to provide the rhymes. After printing out the text, they can illustrate the passage and draw the rhymes.

Present the children with selections of Clue Cards, four Rhyme Word Cards which rhyme with the Clue Cards, and one which does not. Ask the children to find all the rhyming words. They should be encouraged to use the shared spelling patterns from the Clue Cards to help them. The children can then be encouraged to read the rhymes and can match the appropriate Rhyme Picture Cards to the Rhyme Word Cards. **AA SR2.**

Use selections of four Rhyme Picture Cards which rhyme and their matching Rhyme Word Cards and two or three Rhyme Word Cards which are not in the same rhyme family. Spread the Rhyme Word Cards face-up over the table and give the Rhyme Picture Cards to the children. Ask them to find and read the rhyming word to match each picture. The teacher can have the Clue Card and be the first to find a match. The children can then be encouraged to use the Clue Card as a clue to help them to find the other rhyming words. The aim of this activity is to help the children realise that the rhyming words have a shared spelling pattern and that therefore they can use the spelling pattern of the Clue Card to help them to find and read the other rhyming words. **AA**

Play a 'rhyming list' game. Use a selection of Rhyming Picture Cards. Write lists of matching rhyming words, with the shared spelling patterns underneath each other, on strips of card, one for each player. Players take turns at taking a card from the pile. The player then has to say what the picture is, find that word on their list and put a counter on it. The winner is the first person to get a counter on all the words on their list. **SR6, SR7.**

■ The number of lists and thus the number of rhyming families can be increased.

Make 'rhyme dice'. Use two cubes and write the shared spelling pattern of six rhyming families on one and the onsets of the rhyming family words on the other. Children take turns to throw the two dice and to read the word made by placing the dice with the onset of the word in front of the other dice with the rime. The child can then say whether the word is a real word or a nonsense word. **SR2**.

■ Alternatively, a game can be played by using the Rhyme Picture Cards which match the words made by the dice and placing them face-up on the table. The first person to throw each rhyme word and read it, collects the matching picture card and keeps it. The winner is the person with the most cards at the end.

⁄ Use a selection of Rhyme Word Cards. Spread the cards face-down in front of the children. Children take turns to pick a card and to read the word on it. They then have to think of a word which rhymes with the word on the card. **SR3**, **SR9**.

■ As an extension activity, the children can have a go at spelling the rhyming word that they have just thought of on a chalk board, wipe-board or in a sand tray. They should be encouraged to use the spelling pattern of the rhyme word on the card that they have chosen to help them.

Building in progression

You can adapt all of these games and activities to build in progression, as well as adapting them to the specific onsets and rhymes used in each Story Rhyme. Progression can be introduced by using the same game orally or using letters, or by segmenting both onsets and rimes. In general, the levels of difficulty are:

Onsets

1 oral game – single phonemes only
2 game matching single phonemes to letters
3 oral game – double-consonant onsets
4 game matching double-consonant onsets to letters
5 oral game – segmenting double-consonant onsets
6 game segmenting spellings for double-consonant onsets

Rhymes and Analogies

1 oral game – simple rhymes (Rhyme Picture Cards)
2 same game with spelling (Rhyme Word Cards)
3 game with Rhyme Picture Cards, matched to Rhyme Word Cards
4 game with Rhyme Word Cards, matched to Rhyme Picture Cards
5 game with Rhyme Word Cards, child has to write an analogous word on a wipe board
6 game with Rhyme Picture Cards, child has to write rhymes on a wipe board

Dear

Your child has been given the story ....
....
....
to bring home to share with you. We are using this story as a fun way to
learn about rhyme.

Please could you read the story with your child. Please stress the rhyming
words as you read. Spend a few minutes helping your child to think up new
words to rhyme with ....

Read the story again, and ask your child to tell you the rhyming words
They can use the pictures to help them.

This practice with rhyme will be very helpful to your child's reading. Thank
you very much.

Dear

Your child has been given the story . . . .

. . . .

. . . .

to bring home to share with you. We are using this story as a fun way to learn about spellings for rhyming words.

Please read the story to your child, asking them to finger-point to words which rhyme with . . . . If they point

to the wrong word, show them the correct one. But don't interrupt the flow of the story.

After reading the story, ask your child to show you the rhyming words. Talk about the shared spelling patterns that make up the rhyming sounds in the words. For example, ... in the words . . . .

If they can't point to the rhymes while you are reading, go back to the rhyme words later. Stress the first sound in the word. Help your child to find the first letter or letters. Show them that these letters always match the first sounds.

This practice with spelling and sound will be very helpful to your child's reading. Thank you very much.

Dear

Your child has been given the story . . . .

. . . .

. . . .

to bring home to share with you. We are using this story as a fun way to learn about spelling patterns for rhymes.

Please ask your child to read you the story. Ask them to finger-point to each word as they read. They should move their finger to each new word as they say it.

If they start pointing to the wrong words, let them finish the story. Then go back to the parts where they got confused. Stress the first sound in the words, and help them to find the first letter or letters. Show them that they can work out where they should be pointing because the first letters in words match the first sounds.

Now ask them to go through the story again, pointing out the spelling patterns for the rhyming words. For example, the . . . . in the words . . . . Then help your child to think of some more words that rhyme with the key words in the story. These words are . . . .

. . . .

You could also write the key words at the top of a sheet of paper. Then ask your child to write the new rhyming words under the correct key word. Show them that the spelling patterns for the rhymes are always the same.

This practice with spelling and sound will be very helpful to your child's reading. Thank you very much.

The Story Rhymes: summary checklist

1 Introducing the Story Rhyme

■ Read through the Story Rhyme, emphasising the rhymes. Point to the spelling patterns, and any rhymes in pictures.

■ Go through the story more slowly, verse by verse. Focus on the rhyming words, using guided response questions.

■ Check comprehension of the narrative structure, using guided response questions.

■ Reinforce the phonological patterns in the Story Rhymes, in the sequence onset, rhyme, analogy.

2 Onset work

■ Begin with oral work based on the Story Rhyme.

■ Extend by linking sounds to letters.

3 Rhyme work

■ Begin with oral work based on the Story Rhyme.

■ Extend by linking sounds to letters.

4 Using analogies

■ Play the Clue Game.

■ Extend by using word-family approach and segmenting longer words.

5 Link to other curriculum areas

The Clue Game: summary checklist

- Put the Clue Card at the top of the board.
- Make the clue word from plastic letters, separating onset and rime.

Reading

- Add a new rhyming word, separated into onset and rime, lining up the spelling pattern with the clue.
- Ask the children for the sound of the onset (they can use the Alphabet Frieze).
- Ask the children for the sound of the rime (they can use the clue word).
- Ask them to read the new word for you.
- Ask them how they can check that they are right (they can use analogies).

Spelling

- Ask the children for a new word to spell.
- Ask them how to write its rime (they can use the clue word).
- Ask them how to write the onset (they can use the Alphabet Frieze).
- Ask them how they can check that they are right (they can use analogies).

- Make the clue word at the top of the board.
- Leave a gap between onset and rime.

Reading

- Add a new onset word, separated into onset and rime, lining up the spelling pattern of the onset with the clue.
- Ask the children for the sound of the onset.

Then either:

- Ask the children if they can think of a clue for the rime.
- Ask them to read the new word for you.

Or:

- Tell them the whole word.
- Ask them how they can check the beginning sound (they can use analogies).

Spelling

- Ask the children for a new word to spell.
- Ask them how to write its onset (they can use the clue word).
- Ask them how they can check that they are right (they can use analogies).
- If they think of a word with a familiar rime, ask them how to spell the rime using a Clue Card.

net

cat

zip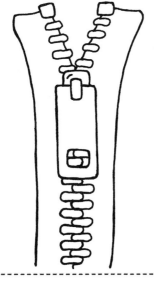

pin

fan

bed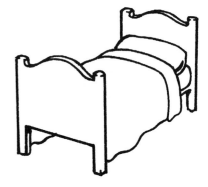

tub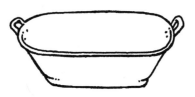

dog

cap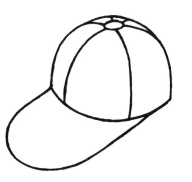

sad

hen

hit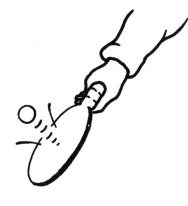

lid

leg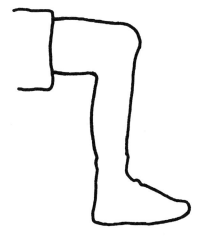

nut

sun

jam

swim

wig

crab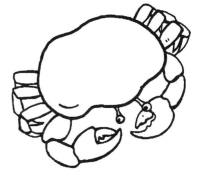

shop

knot

hay

bell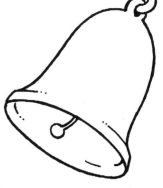

bag

ball

hill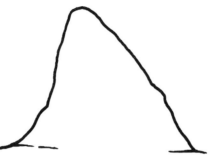

snow

duck

star

mum

knob

clock

sack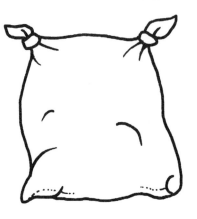

king

long

plug

brush

flash

dress

112

chick

grass

bang

kiss

puff

stung

cross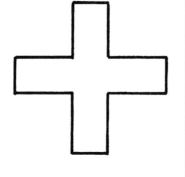

cliff

113

A **a**	B **b**	C **c**	D **d**	E **e**
F **f**	G **g**	H **h**	I **i**	J **j**
K **k**	L **l**	M **m**	N **n**	O **o**
P **p**	Q **q**	R **r**	S **s**	T **t**
U **u**	V **v**	W **w**	X **x**	Y **y**
Z **z**	**ch**	**sh**	**th**	**wh**

Use for letter bingo or lotto, or to make alphabet strips.

Cut out the boxes and place them in a pile with the larger box at the bottom. Write onsets on the right edge of the smaller boxes, and the rime on the right of the larger box. The child then 'flips' the onset to create new words by joining them up with the rime. The child can draw pictures of the words on the left of the boxes when they have read the words, or on the backs of the pages as a memory aid.

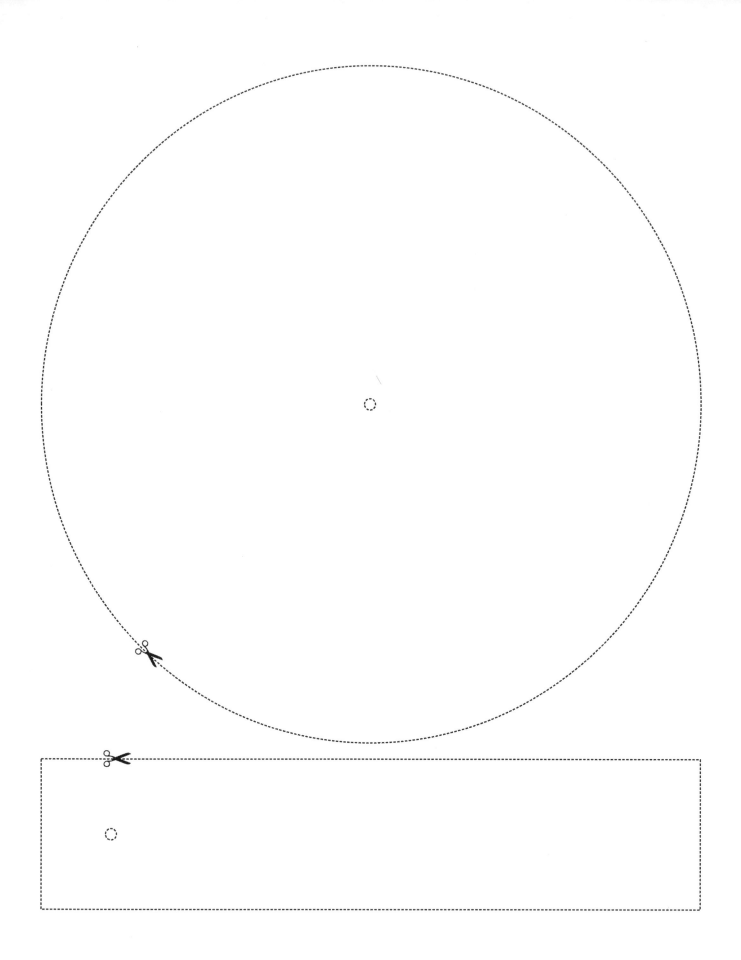

Use a butterfly clip to attach the pointer to the back of the wheel at the point marked with a dot. Write onsets around the wheel. Write a rime on the right of the pointer. The child turns the wheel to create new words by joining up onsets and rimes.

Use the Rhyme and Analogy Card Game cards or the Alphabet strips on page 114 to create Bingo games. Stick two sheets together to make larger boards and enlarge or reduce the sheet on a photocopier as necessary.

Start

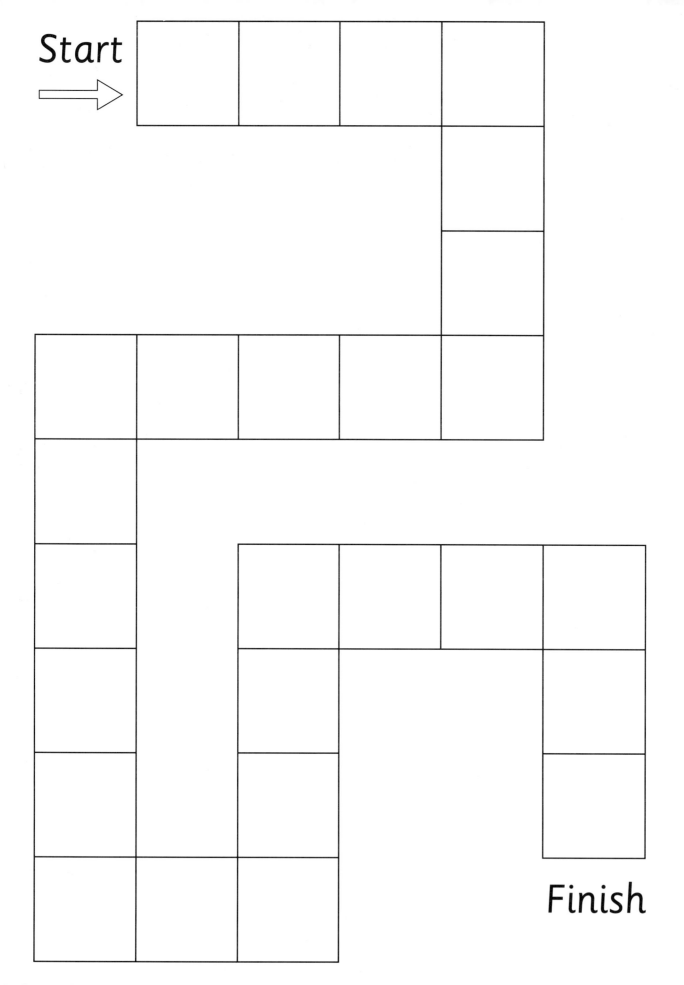

Finish

Pick a card and move on only if you can say the sound that the letter makes or that the picture begins with. If using rhyme cards, move on only if you can think of a word which rhymes with the picture or word on the card. Alternatively, write words or draw pictures in the boxes. Move by thinking of a word that rhymes with or begins with the same letter as the item in the box

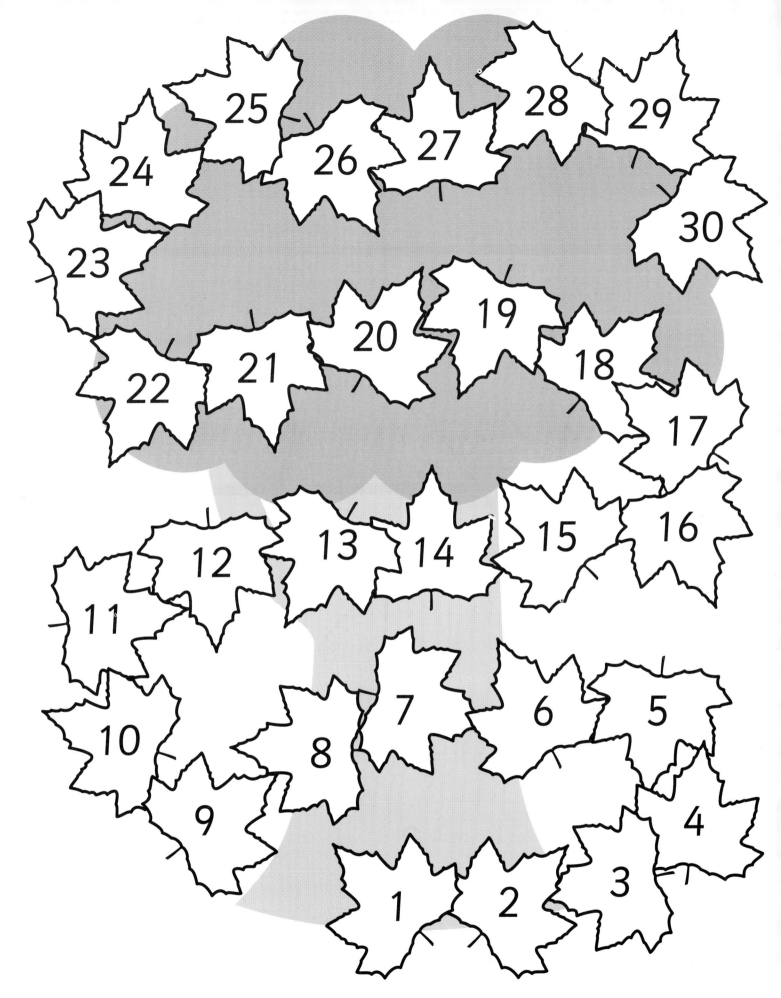

Pick a card and move on only if you can say the sound that the letter makes or that the picture begins with. If using rhyme cards, move on only if you can think of a word which rhymes with the picture or word on the card.

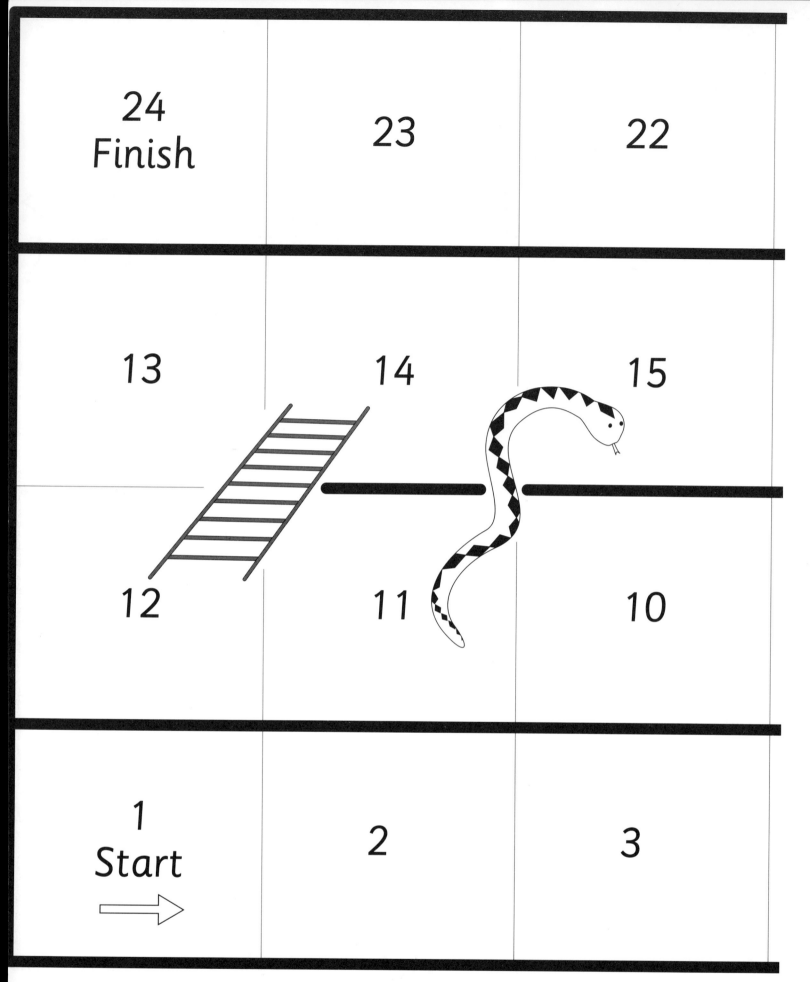

24 Finish	23	22
13	14	15
12	11	10
1 Start →	2	3

Attach to a copy of page 121 to create a large board. Pick a card. Move on if you can say the sound or rhyme on the card

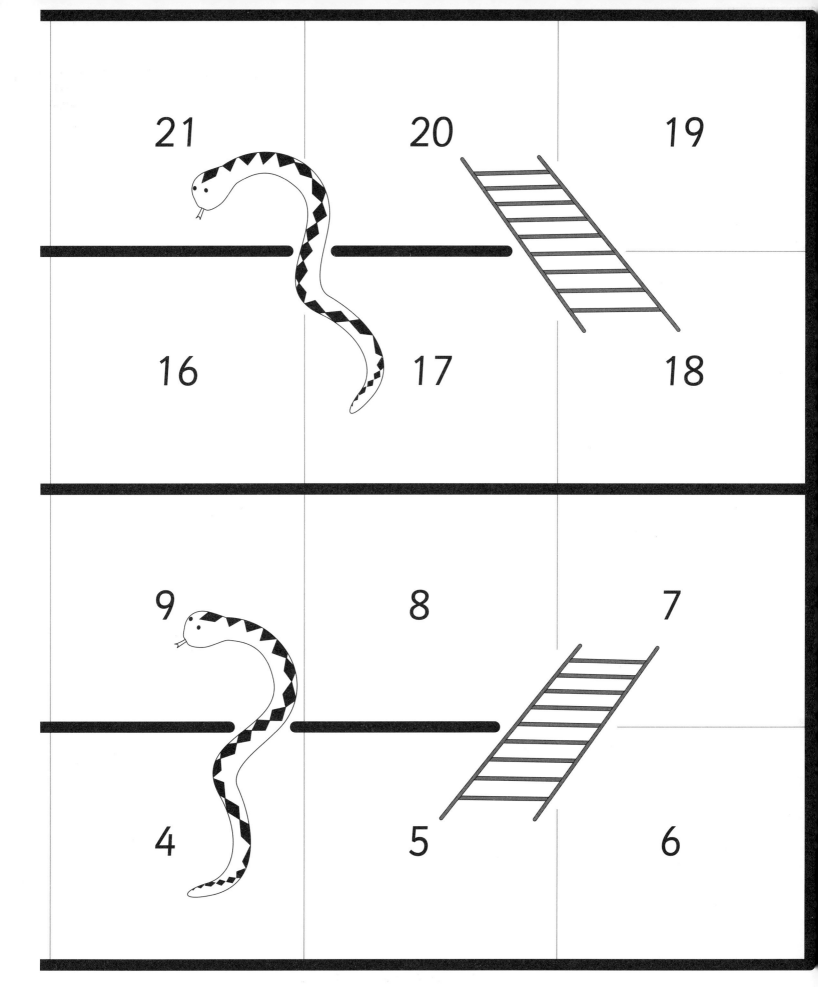

Attach to a copy of page 120 to create a large board. Pick a card. Move on if you can say the sound or rhyme on the card

Write a Clue Card word on the centre piece and rhyming words on the jigsaw pieces. Use the outline for one rhyme family initially, then create separate jigsaws for a number of families and mix the pieces together to make a more difficult game.

Write the clue word at the top. Write a rhyming word on each line, adding other letters before and after. The child searches for the rhyming words. Write the words on the bottom of the sheet, on the back, or on a separate sheet, to help the child if necessary.

Research background to Rhyme and Analogy

Rhyming and reading

For most children, a sensitivity to rhyme is an early developing skill. The Russian psychologist Chukovsky noted that children as young as 18 months of age 'jabbered' rhymed nonsense for hours, talking to themselves in rhymed syllables ('alia, valia, dalia, malia . . . '). He described young children as 'avid creators of word rhythms and rhymes'.

The ability to *reflect* on this knowledge about rhyme – to become 'aware' of having it – is usually present by age three. Most three-year-olds can judge whether 'Jill' rhymes with 'hill', or whether 'cat' rhymes with 'hat'. Longitudinal research studies that have followed children's progress over a number of years have shown that rhyming skill is a strong predictor of later success in reading and spelling. This link appears to hold even when factors such as IQ and mother's educational level (an approximate index of social class) are controlled.

Studies that have provided training in rhyme have shown that explicit training in rhyme awareness can help a child's reading and spelling development. This is especially true when rhyme training is accompanied by teaching about the alphabet. Furthermore, children who are poor at making judgements about rhyme often turn out to have reading difficulties. Recent estimates suggest that around 80 per cent of dyslexic children have primarily phonological, rather than visual, deficits.

Rhyme and alliteration also seem to be especially *salient* for young children. Phonological judgements about whether words begin with the same sound, or share rhymes, are fairly easy for children even before they begin school. Judgements that involve smaller units of sound – phonemes – are more difficult. A *phoneme* is the smallest unit of sound that changes the meaning of a word. 'Tip' and 'top' differ by a single phoneme, the middle phoneme, and 'tip' and 'tin' differ by the final phoneme. 'Tip' and 'sip' differ by a single initial phoneme. This initial phonemic difference is the only one that is easy for most children to hear. Most children will find it difficult to tell you whether 'hip' and 'lit' share a middle sound, or whether 'hop' and 'tap' end with the same sound. This kind of *phonemic* judgement is very difficult for children until they have attained a certain level of reading. So it is important to begin teaching a child at the appropriate developmental level – the level of rhyme and alliteration.

Teaching at the correct phonological level

Why should rhyming be so important for *reading*, which involves learning about alphabetic letters? The reason seems to be that categorising words on the basis of rhyme gives children access to two useful linguistic units within English syllables. These are the linguistic units of the *onset* and the *rime*.

Any syllable can be divided into its onset and rime by segmenting it at the vowel. The *onset* in spoken words corresponds to any initial consonants in the syllable, and the *rime* corresponds to the vowel and any following consonants. The onset in 'Jill' corresponds to the sound 'j', and the onset in 'hot' corresponds to the 'h'. The rime in 'Jill' corresponds to the spelling pattern 'ill', and the rime in 'hot' is 'ot'. Words such as 'at' and 'and' have no onset, consisting only of a rime.

Onsets can be longer than a single letter, however, just like most rimes. The onset in 'spill' corresponds to the spelling unit SP, and the onset in 'spring' corresponds to the spelling unit SPR. Research has shown that onsets and rimes are psychologically very accessible to beginning readers. As onset and rime units seem to be phonologically 'natural' units for young children, the onset–rime level would appear to be a useful level at which to start teaching children about spelling–sound correspondences.

Teaching children the correspondences between onsets, rimes, and spelling patterns is *not* quite the same thing as traditional phonics, however. Traditional 'phonic' reading schemes are built around the *phoneme*. There are a number of drawbacks to using a phonemic method with *beginning* readers. One is that children have great difficulty in hearing the constituent phonemes in spoken words. Phonemes are not readily accessible units of sound to young children, unless they are in the initial position in the word. Another is that the correspondence between phonemes and alphabetic letters is not always one-to-one. In fact, in some words, such as 'light', 'sheep', and 'snow', there is no one-to-one correspondence between letters and sounds. It is very difficult to segment words into phonemes simply by looking at their spelling patterns.

A third problem for beginning readers who are taught to read by using a phonemic strategy is memory capacity. Young children have fairly limited verbal memories, and the sequential requirements of segmentation, sound generation, and blending may be beyond the beginning reader.

Starting off at the onset–rime level avoids many of these problems. Onsets and rimes are very accessible phonological units for beginning readers. In fact, most children can segment spoken words into onsets and rimes before they start school, and some can even segment multi-syllabic words into their constituent onsets and rimes (as in *w-ig-w-am*). The correspondence between oral onsets and rimes and the matching spelling sequences in written words is relatively easy for a child to work out, as the segmentation is always at the vowel. Finally, a child who is using onsets and rimes only needs to remember the sounds of two units at any one time: the sound of the onset (the 'j' for 'Jill', or the 'l' for 'light'), and the sound of the rime (the 'ill' for 'Jill', and the 'ight' for 'light'). This is well within the capability of most children.

However, the problems with a phonemic approach to reading do not mean that it is wrong to teach children the most common sounds of the alphabet letters. In fact, it is crucial to do so. Children's difficulty in hearing single phonemes within words does not apply when the phoneme is at the beginning of a word, i.e. when it is an onset. Preschoolers should have no difficulty in telling you that 'Jill' and 'jump' begin with the same sound, or that 'chip' and 'chop' sound the same at the beginning. These sounds (onsets) should be taught explicitly, as should the double-letter single-phoneme onsets 'ch', 'sh', 'th', and 'wh', which are actually single sounds.

The consistency of rime spelling patterns

Perhaps the biggest advantage of an initial focus on onsets and rimes, however, is that children who pay attention to rime spelling patterns will find written English far more *consistent* in its spelling–sound correspondence than children who pay attention to phonemes.

Written English has the reputation of being highly ambiguous in the way that it represents sound. Although this ambiguity has been the focus of countless spelling reformers over the centuries, spelling–sound ambiguity in English is largely at the phonemic level. Written English is actually quite *consistent* at the onset-rime level.

This can be illustrated by thinking about vowel sounds. The chief source of variability in written English is always the vowel. The vowel A can have different pronunciations in the words 'cat', 'ball', and 'grass', and changes its sound again in words like 'wave' and 'late'. The vowel O has different pronunciations in the words 'hot', 'one', and 'lord', and changes its sound again in 'cold' and 'hole'. Similar examples could be found for E, I, and U. In most cases, the sound of the vowel changes as the final consonant or consonants change. The same is true of vowel digraphs (think of EA in 'pear', 'pearl', and 'peach').

Most of this variability in vowel pronunciation is removed by considering the *families* of the words that share these rimes (cat, bat, hat, mat . . . , ball, fall, hall, wall . . . , grass, class, glass . . . , each, peach, teach. . . .). Rhyme families share final consonants as well as vowels. Within most rime families, therefore, vowel pronunciation is very predictable. When it is not, there is often only a single exception to the rime, which can be pointed out by the teacher (gave, wave, save – *have*). Alternatively, there may be a whole group of consistent rhyming exceptions, which form a sub-family of their own (pear, bear, wear – hear, near, dear, etc.).

Furthermore, many rime families are extremely large. For example, a simple word like 'pin' has many *neighbours* (in, win, tin, chin, bin, din, grin, twin, fin, skin, thin, spin, etc.). In fact, if we include neighbours with more than one syllable, then there are 884 words in written English that share the spelling pattern 'in' with 'pin' (winter, finish, begin, robin, etc.). There are 904 neighbours for the rime 'en' in 'ten', 750 neighbours for the rime 'an' in 'fan', and 1,908 neighbours for the rime 'er' in 'her' (although these are multisyllabic words, like 'water', 'never', 'person', and 'jersey').

A focus on rime may also remove some apparent spelling–sound 'irregularities' completely. For example, the word 'light' is seen as an irregular word, because the sounds of its constituent letters do not add up to the sound of the whole word. Sounding out 'light' letter by letter is certainly a bad strategy for reading it. Yet there are 90 other words in written English that use the 'ight' spelling sequence for the rime in 'light' (right, might, light, night, bright, sight, fight, flight, tight, slight, sunlight, tonight, etc.). So this irregularity in letter–sound correspondence *disappears* when we think about onsets and rimes.

These dual advantages of *consistency of pronunciation* and *family size* are two good reasons for teaching children about the spelling–sound correspondences for rimes. In all, there are about 616 rime families that describe the English spelling system. However, this does not mean that we need to teach children *all* of the rime spellings that they will come across when reading and writing English. This would be repetitive and boring. A better goal is to give children a *strategy* for attacking new words that exploits a phonological distinction (rhyme) that is very accessible to them. This strategy is *analogy*.

Analogies between rhyming words

Research on the spontaneous reading behaviour of young children first drew our attention to the importance of analogies in reading development. An analogy in reading involves using the spelling pattern of a word that you know in order to read a word that you don't know.

For example, a child who knows how to read the word 'Jill' should be able to work out how to read words like 'hill' and 'pill' for herself, as long as she knows the pronunciation of the onsets 'h' and 'p'. A child who knows the word 'king' should be able to work out how to read words like 'wing', 'sing', and 'ring', as long as she knows the onsets 'w', 's', and 'r'. This child will also know an important spelling unit for reading bisyllabic words like 'walking', 'singing', and 'reading'.

The analogy research found that some children made these connections spontaneously when reading new words. The analogies that these children made were most likely to be based on shared spelling patterns that reflected the *rime*, as in 'king' and 'wing', or 'Jill' and 'hill'. Although some children could also see connections between words that shared spelling segments at the beginning, like 'bean', 'bead' and 'beat', the most salient analogies, and those that developed earliest, were rime analogies.

The analogy research also found that the most important variable in spontaneous analogy use was the *level* of a child's rhyming skills. Children who made many spontaneous analogies in reading were those with strong rhyming skills. Children with poor rhyming skills found it difficult to use analogies. However, other research has shown that even these children can learn to use rime analogies with explicit help. The first step in providing this explicit help turns out to be to develop their *phonological* skills. Ensuring a good oral foundation of phonological skills at the onset–rime level is therefore crucial if all children are to be taught to use analogies.

Beyond the spontaneous use of analogy

Some children will use analogies spontaneously once they have good phonological skills, but others will not. More recent analogy research has shown that most children can learn to use analogies through explicit teaching, even those children with reading difficulties. Although a good phonological foundation comes first, it is also important to model the analogy strategy explicitly if we wish to teach *all* children how to make analogies.

The most successful research studies on teaching reading by analogy have used a word 'families' approach. As noted above, whole groups or families of words in English share the same spelling pattern for a particular rhyming sound, and some of these families are very large. In order to use analogies to read words in these families, children only need to remember one example of a relevant spelling pattern. This is the 'clue' word for the analogy.

One way of helping children to remember clue words is to have them permanently on display in the classroom. In this way, their spelling patterns are always available. These key words can then be used as 'clues' to reading and spelling new words when the children are working by themselves. This idea was first introduced in research by Irene Gaskins, who used a 'word wall' to display key words for dyslexic readers. Most reading-by-analogy training studies have incorporated similar wall displays, as forgetting the 'clue' words can be a real problem for children, and especially for backward readers. A picture mnemonic can further aid retention of key spelling patterns. Finally, another pioneer in teaching reading by analogy, Patricia Cunningham, advocates teaching poorer readers to chant analogous spelling patterns aloud ('If n-i-n-e is nine, s-p-i-n-e must be spine'), as a further aid to developing spelling memory.

Conclusions

The conclusions that can be drawn from recent research on reading by analogy are thus fairly simple ones from the point of view of teaching.

- The first is that phonological skills are very important for reading progress. Phonological skills are most easily developed by giving all children a good oral grounding in rhyme and alliteration.
- The second is that children should be made aware of the linguistic units of the onset and the rime, initially at an oral level. These units will be important for using analogies in reading.
- The third is that children should be explicitly taught to make analogies between shared spelling patterns in words. They need to be shown how to segment words at the vowel, and blend new onsets onto shared rimes.
- The fourth is that children who get lots of examples of rime analogies will find it easier to learn the analogy strategy. The word-family approach ensures that children learn lots of examples of words sharing the same rimes.

Finally, it can be very motivating for children to realise that they can work out how to read quite long words because they know the different rime families corresponding to each syllable. Words like 'nightingale' and 'lemonade' have syllables made up of rimes from highly frequent families, and longer words like these can also be read by analogy. However, in order to become good readers and spellers of written English, children must eventually progress from onset–rime units to phonemes. Although onsets and rimes are a good place to begin to learn about reading and writing, phonemic knowledge is the eventual goal of the fluent reader.

Further reading

Research

ADAMS, M. J. (1990), *Beginning to Read: Thinking and Learning about Print*, Cambridge, Mass: MIT Press.

BEARD, R. (1995), *Rhyme, Reading and Writing*. London: Hodder & Stoughton Educational.

BRYANT, P. E., and BRADLEY, L. (1985), *Children's Reading Problems*, Oxford: Basil Blackwell.

GOSWAMI, U., and BRYANT, P. E. (1990), *Phonological Skills and Learning to Read*, Hove: Lawrence Erlbaum Associates.

GOUGH, P., EHRI, L., and TREIMAN, R. (1992), *Reading Acquisition*, Hillsdale, NJ: Lawrence Erlbaum Associates.

Teaching

CUNNINGHAM, P. M. (1992), *Phonics They Use: Words for Reading and Writing*, 2nd ed.; New York: Harper Collins College Publishers.

DOWNER, M. A., and GASKINS, I. W. (1986), *Benchmark Word Identification/Vocabulary Development Programme*, Media, Pa: Benchmark Press.

HENDERSON, E. (1990), *Teaching Spelling*, Boston: Houghton Mifflin.

JAMES, F., and KERR, A. (1993), *On First Reading: Ideas for Developing Reading Skills with Children from Four to Seven*, Twickenham: Belair Publications.

HOLDAWAY, D. (1980), *Independence in Reading*, Portsmouth, NH: Heinemann.

WAGSTAFF, J. M. (1995), *Phonics that Work! New Strategies for the Reading/Writing Classroom*, New York: Scholastic Professional Books.

Glossary

Alliteration: shared beginning sounds in words.

Analogy: the use of one word as a basis for working out the pronunciation or the spelling of a word with the same rime.

Assonance: shared medial sounds in words, usually reflecting shared vowel sounds.

Digraph: a single sound represented by two letters in spelling, e.g. 'sh'.

Onset: technically the *sound* in any syllable that corresponds to the consonant/s at the beginning of the syllable. Used here to refer to spelling patterns for initial consonants or consonant clusters. A multisyllabic word can have more than one onset (**valentine**).

Phoneme: the smallest unit of sound that changes the meaning of a word.

Phonemic awareness*: the ability to recognise *phonemes*.

Phonological awareness: the ability to recognise and manipulate shared sounds in words.

Rime: technically, the *sound* in any syllable that corresponds to the vowel and any following consonant/s in that syllable. Used here to refer to spelling patterns for rhymes. A multisyllabic word can have more than one rime (**val-en-tine**).